Textile Traditions of Indonesia

Mary Hunt Kahlenberg

Los Angeles County Museum of Art

Front and back cover:
Palepai, Sumatra
catalog no. 8

Library of Congress Cataloging
in Publication Data
Kahlenberg, Mary Hunt.
Textile traditions of Indonesia.

Includes bibliographies.
1. Textile fabrics—Indonesia.
2. Folk art—Indonesia.
I. Los Angeles Co., Calif. Museum of Art,
Los Angeles. II. Title
NK8880.A1K33 746 09598 77-17884
ISBN 0-87587-083-X

Published by the
Los Angeles County Museum of Art
5905 Wilshire Boulevard
Los Angeles, California 90036

Copyright © 1977 by
Museum Associates of the
Los Angeles County Museum of Art

Book designed by Denis Parkhurst.
Composed in Garamond types
by R S Typographics.
Printed in Los Angeles by
Gardner/Fulmer.

Contents

4   Trustees and Supervisors

5   Acknowledgments

7   Introduction

9   Glossary

13   Color Plates

Catalog   25   Sumatra

41   Borneo

53   Celebes

59   Java

73   Bali

79   Sumba

87   Flores

95   Lomblen

97   Roti, Ndao, Savu

105   Timor

108   Kisar

109   Sumbawa

110   Other Indonesian Textiles in the Los Angeles County Museum of Art

114   Bibliographies

Acknowledgments

The richness and strong visual force of Indonesian textiles have always held great appeal for me. Although these cloths have long been appreciated by the textile historians, anthropologists, and art historians working in the Southeast Asian area, they had never gained popularity with the more general public. The most obvious reason is that pieces of extremely fine quality have not been on public view until the past few years, when exhibitions of Indonesian textiles in the Museum of Fine Arts, Boston; The Textile Museum in Washington, D.C.; and The Honolulu Academy of Fine Arts in Hawaii have begun to draw attention to this incredible material.

Only a few years ago there was just a handful of good quality Indonesian textiles in the Los Angeles County Museum of Art collection. In 1972 I had the opportunity of visiting several of the major Dutch Indonesian collections. Excited by what I saw, I convinced the department's support group, the Costume Council, to partially sponsor a trip to Indonesia and to provide funds for acquisitions. This was the beginning of a serious collection that has continued to grow with the Council's support. In the past year additional funds from the Board of Trustees have made possible the purchase of important pieces not previously represented in the collection.

There is never enough time to prepare an exhibition or a catalog, but enthusiasm over this project has helped us accomplish a great deal very quickly. Many people have helped and I appreciate it tremendously. First is the staff of the Textiles and Costumes Department—Florence Karant, Nola Ewing, and Janice McGruder—who have had to continue their daily work while developing expertise about Indonesia, including the spelling and meaning of many Indonesian words. The staff of the Textile Conservation Department, under Fernande Jones, informed me that textiles from this area are particularly soiled, but they have been seduced by the beauty beneath. Kristen McCormick of the registrar's office has assisted with loans. Several loyal department volunteers have helped with research and cataloging, including Dale Gluckman, Phyllis Guy, Mary Kefgen, Dorothy Laupa, Lorraine Olson, and Mary Jane Leland, who spent countless hours helping with captions and other details.

My very special thanks go to the eight authors of the catalog: Steven G. Alpert, James J. Fox, Dr. Mattiebelle Gittinger, Jeff Holmgren and Anita Spertus, Garrett and Bronwen Solyom, and Kent Watters. They have added their knowledge to this catalog in their own areas of specialty, giving it far more depth than if all areas had been covered by a single author. The editing of these diverse texts by authors traveling thousands of miles away has been most adeptly done by Nancy Grubb and Jeanne D'Andrea.

I am also grateful to the museums and private lenders. Their textiles added a dimension and totality to the exhibition that would not have been possible in such a young collection. My thanks to Steven G. Alpert, Highland Park, Illinois; Angus MacFie Gallery, West Los Angeles; Don R. Bierlich, Pacific Basin Services, Los Angeles; Gordon Bishop, Bishop International, New York; The Brooklyn Museum, New York; Cooper Hewitt Museum of Decorative Arts and Design, New York; Professor Samuel Eilenberg, London and New York; Joseph Fischer, Berkeley; James J. Fox, Holland; Jeff Holmgren and Anita Spertus, New York; Indianapolis Museum of Art, Indiana; Mary Jane Leland, Los Angeles; The Metropolitan Museum of Art, New York; Museum of Cultural History, University of California, Los Angeles; Peabody Museum, Salem, Massachusetts; Terry Saklofsky, Vancouver, British Columbia; The Textile Museum, Washington, D.C.; Kent Watters, Bali, Indonesia; and Michael Yerby, Berkeley.

The exhibition would not have been possible without a matching fund grant from The Home Silk Shop. I wish to thank Murry Pepper, president of The Home Silk Shop, for his support and also the following people who helped to support the catalog: Angus MacFie Gallery, West Los Angeles; Baumann & Kaplan; Don R. Bierlich, Pacific Basin Services; Casa de las Tejedoras, Santa Ana, California; Ethnic Arts Council; The Fashion Group, Inc.; Fultheim Imports; Max and Rita Lawrence; William R. Merzbach; Raymond & Keith Antiques; Jay and Judy Schuster; Southern California Handweavers Guild, Inc.; Kent Watters; and a special thanks again for the continuing support of our Costume Council.

Mary Hunt Kahlenberg
Curator, Textiles and Costumes

VIET NAM

ACEH

LAKE TOBA

WEST MALAYSIA

Malacca

Singapore

SUMATRA

Palembang

Bengkulen

LAMPONG

Krōe

Jakarta

Pekalongan

Lasem

JAVA

Cirebon

BALI

Tenganan

Jogjakarta

Surakarta

NUSA PENIDA

LOMBOK

SUMBAWA

SUMBA

SAVU

BORNEO

SARAWAK

SABAH

KALIMANTAN

RONGKONG

CELEBES

GALUMPANG

Makassar

SIKKA

FLORES

Endeh

Introduction

Mary Hunt Kahlenberg

The chain of Indonesian islands, which stretches from the Malay Peninsula to Australia, is the home of one of the most sumptuous and original textile traditions in the world. For Indonesians the art of weaving—the intercrossing of the warp and the weft—symbolizes the structure of the cosmos: the warp threads fastened between the ends of the loom represent the predestined elements of life; the weft passing in and out and back and forth denotes life's variables.

For centuries the production of textiles for daily and ceremonial use has been the work of women, part of the overall pattern of their lives. Many textiles take several years to complete, for production is not a continuous process, but rather one that fits into the daily rhythm. Only during certain periods of the year when tending crops is not necessary can women devote their time to weaving. Cotton (the most commonly used fiber) must be carded and spun; ikat warps must be stretched and bound. This work is done on the porch or in the shade of the overhanging roof, allowing the women to remain in touch with the other activities around them. Materials for natural dyes must be gathered and prepared, and once this is done the dyeing itself may take several days or even months of work and waiting before the desired rich colors are achieved. In some cases an entire agricultural cycle will pass between the various dye baths, with another color added each year. A textile made in such a laborious manner may serve as a ceremonial garment for many generations, or it may be included as part of a burial gift where its existence is believed to be eternal. The idea of waiting several years for a finished product, and the sense of timeless continuity this suggests, is incompatible with our more rigidly structured Western concept of time; yet it is an essential element of the Indonesian culture that began in ancient times.

During the neolithic period (beginning 2000 B.C.) emigrants from Southeast Asia reached Indonesia, bringing with them the Australian languages. Present-day Indonesian linguistic structure and racial characteristics have their origins in this time, although different cultures have developed throughout the archipelago. A strong influence came from China at the end of the first millennium B.C. as traders began exchanging Chinese finished goods for local Indonesian agricultural products. These Chinese objects, including many bronze weapons, exhibited the rich decorative style that had flourished for thousands of years in China. Basically curvilinear and spiraling forms that had their origin in the tendrils and stems of plants, these designs continued in the fantastically stylized animal motifs of the Iban textiles of Borneo. By the first century A.D. Indian trade contacts stimulated the development of Hindu kingdoms throughout Java. Today, Hinduism remains strong in Bali, where the textiles show a close connection to those of India. Brightly colored brocades enriched with gold and silver continue the sumptuous Indian textile tradition, and the *geringsing,* or double-ikat textiles, woven in the Balinese village of Tenganan are closely related in technique and design to cloths woven in western India. Toward the end of the thirteenth century the spread of Islam began in Sumatra, reaching Java and other islands in the fifteenth and sixteenth centuries. Various styles of metallic brocade, particularly those of Sumatra and Sumbawa, continue an opulent and formal tradition that appears in textiles of the Islamic areas of India, Iran, and North Africa. When the Portuguese, English, and Dutch came seeking spices in the sixteenth century, they contributed a repertoire of realistic floral designs, particularly popular on Javanese batiks. Heraldic images such as the rampant lion were adapted from European coins and remain a prestigious symbol in Sumbanese textiles.

Despite the diverse outside influences they have absorbed in varying degrees, the islands of Indonesia share many social and religious practices. The primary social and political organization is the clan, which is divided into distinct groups of "nobles," "freemen," and "slaves." These three groups live within a village or city unit, presided over by a member of the nobility. Clan life is punctuated by ceremonies connected to the view of life as a series of inevitable stages, including birth, puberty, marriage, and death. People gather from great distances for these ceremonies, wearing costumes that identify their family and social rank. Specified numbers and types of textiles are exchanged as gifts as part of the rituals, and in some areas large textiles are hung that signify rank or that contain symbolism pertinent to the event. The widespread ancestor cult is reflected in extravagant funeral and death rites. Special garments that contain symbols to guide the spirit to the next life are buried with the corpse.

Although similar beliefs are shared by many of the peoples throughout Indonesia, distinctive local styles and symbolism have developed from strong community traditions, and often textiles can be identified by their motifs and color as belonging to a certain village. Today there is considerable pressure to alter these traditional forms, as the influence of industrialization begins to break down the conservative religious and social structure. As this severance from tradition destroys the meaning and purpose of the textiles, they are rapidly becoming commercial products rather than symbols of spiritual values. It is therefore vital that at this moment of transition we explore and document the textile traditions. Anthropologists living in Indonesia in recent years and Dutch scholars who traveled there in the late nineteenth and early twentieth centuries have provided valuable information about several of the islands engaged in extensive textile production, but other areas remain sadly undocumented. It is to be hoped that the growing interest stimulated by recent opportunities to see these lavish and graphic textiles will lead to a better understanding of their origins and meanings.

Glossary

A young man from Tenganan wears traditional ceremonial garb, combining geringsing *from Tenganan, a Javanese cotton* batik kain panjang *from central Java, and a* batik silk *slendang from the north coast.*

A Javanese woman applies hot wax to both sides of the cloth with a canting *tool.*

adat — Traditional customs and laws that once regulated every aspect of Indonesian tribal life.

batik — A resist-dyeing technique that involves the alternate waxing and dyeing of cloth. Hot wax is either drawn on with a penlike instrument called a *tulis* or applied with a metal stamp called a *cap*. Both sides of the cloth are waxed. After the first steeping in dye the wax is either boiled or scraped off, and a new application of wax is then made covering the areas previously dyed. The process is repeated until the desired number of colors is achieved, after which all the wax is removed by boiling the cloth in water.

double ikat — An ikat process that requires the binding and dyeing of both the warp and the weft threads. The design is formed when the two sets of threads are woven together.

Garuda — Mythical bird resembling an eagle; the mount of Vishnu, now the official bird of Indonesia.

geringsing — Double-ikat cloth woven only in the small village of Tenganan, East Bali.

ikat — *Ikat* is the stem of the Malay-Indonesian word *mengikat*, meaning "to bind, tie or wind around." The technique involves stretching out the warp or weft threads for a textile, then wrapping a tough vegetable fiber around those areas that are to remain undyed. A separate tying process is required for every color. After the threads are dyed, they are unbound and arranged on the loom for weaving (see illustrations, p. 10).

kain — General word for cloth, but used most specifically to mean an unseamed garment that is wrapped around the body.

kain panjang — Javanese ankle-length skirt cloth, usually worn by women.

kepala — Indonesian word for "head," referring to a panel of contrasting color and design.

9

White warp threads stretched tautly on a frame are tied with strips of dye-proof palm leaf. Areas wrapped with the strips will resist the dye, thus creating an overall white pattern against the dyed background.

Indigo leaves ferment in a pot of water while this Flores woman repeatedly stirs and pours lime powder into another pot prior to the blue dyeing of threads. Organic indigo, rapidly being replaced by synthetic dye, is unpopular with dyers because of its complicated preparation, strong smell, and the permanent stains it leaves on the dyers' hands.

Using the traditional backstrap loom, a Flores woman weaves the ikat-dyed warp threads with a solid color weft thread. It is crucial that the various colored sections of the warp threads be matched precisely in order to create a sharp, clear design.

kombu
Red-brown dye made from the rind of the roots of the *mengkudu* tree (*Morinda citrifolia*).

lau
Sumbanese woman's tubular garment, decorated with ikat and supplementary weft.

naga
Snake or dragon with magical powers associated with the sea and the underworld—a motif frequently used in Indonesian textiles.

pagi-sore
Literally meaning "morning-evening;" refers to batiks divided in half into two different patterns.

palepai
Long ceremonial textiles used in the Lampong area of South Sumatra.

patola
Silk double-ikat textiles exported for several centuries from India throughout Southeast Asia, including Indonesia, where they have been a symbol of status and a major source of design. The luxurious quality and vibrant color of the silk and the foreign origin of the cloths made them highly precious. The most copied type was densely patterned with hexagonal-geometric-floral designs in the center field, a meandering floral side border, and a *tumpal* end border. The double-ikat technique required tying and dyeing both the warp and the weft and painstakingly coordinating the two sets of threads in the weaving process. The exacting nature of this technique demanded careful planning and discipline. The technique is known in Indonesia today only in the Balinese village of Tenganan.

plain weave
The most basic weaving technique, a simple repeat of an over-and-under exposing of the warp and weft. A balanced plain weave shows an equal amount of warp and weft; a warp-faced weave shows a predominant amount of warp; and a weft-faced weave shows a predominant amount of weft.

plangi
Process of applying a design by tying or binding reserve areas prior to immersing the fabric in dye.

prada	Javanese and Balinese application of gold dust, leaf, or paint to a textile.
pua	Iban ceremonial hanging.
ragidup	A Toba Batak (Sumatra) cloth with white end panels that are read as an oracle.
sarong	Rectangular cloth sewn into a tube, worn by both men and women throughout Indonesia.
selimut	Multi-purpose blanket used throughout Indonesia.
slendang	Long, wide shawl worn over the shoulder.
soga	A brown dye used primarily for batik made by combining the bark of the *soga* tree (*Peltophorum pteroccupum*); *backer*, the bark of the *tingi* tree; *sappan* wood; the yellow wood of *Curdriana javanensis Tegerang*; and safflower.
songket	Brocade or supplementary weft techniques, particularly those using metallic threads.
supplementary weave	Technique that involves adding either additional warp or weft threads, which are not integral to the fabric structure and are usually added purely for decorative purposes.
tampan	Small rectangular ceremonial cloth used in the Lampong region of South Sumatra.
tapestry weave	Discontinuous weft weaving, generally covering the warp threads.
tapis	Heavy cotton sarong worn by women in the Lampong region of South Sumatra.
tatibin	Small, narrow ceremonial cloth used in the Lampong region of South Sumatra.
tritik	Process in which design is developed by binding the fabric with tucking, gathering, and other sewing techniques before immersion in the dye.

Patola (*wedding sari*)
Patan, Gujarat, India
Double ikat
Silk
Warp: 449 cm.; weft: 118 cm.
Los Angeles County Museum of Art
Costume Council Fund
M.71.37.2

This Iban woman is weaving an ikat pua *on the porch of a longhouse. Note that since the* pua *is woven one half at a time, only one edge has a striped border.*

Wearing her sarong tube in the traditional over-the-shoulder manner, a Sikka woman carries her basket of produce to the local market.

tumpal   A triangular-shaped pan-Southeast Asian motif, well rep-
          resented in Indonesian art, which may be a blend of
          indigenous and imported elements. *Tumpal* seem
          to be related to growth and fertility, the sacred moun-
          tain Meru, and also perhaps to the tree of life, the lotus,
          and the lotus bud.

twill weave   Characterized by diagonally aligned floats, which are
               warp or weft elements that extend unbound over two or
               more of the opposite warp or weft units.

wayang   Stylized figures based on the characters of myths and
          legends. They appear as textile designs but are best
          known as Javanese shadow puppets.

Note   The Indonesian words used in this catalog are spelled
on Indonesian according to the "new spelling" established by the
Orthography   Indonesian government in August 1972. Among the
              most important changes, *dj* became *j* (e.g., *pandjang*
              became *panjang*), *j* became *y* (e.g., *kebaja* became
              kebaya), and, most difficult for Westerners, *tj* became *c*
              (e.g., *tjap* became *cap*; *tjanting* became *canting,* and
              Tjirebon became *Cirebon*). Note that pronunciation does
              not change.

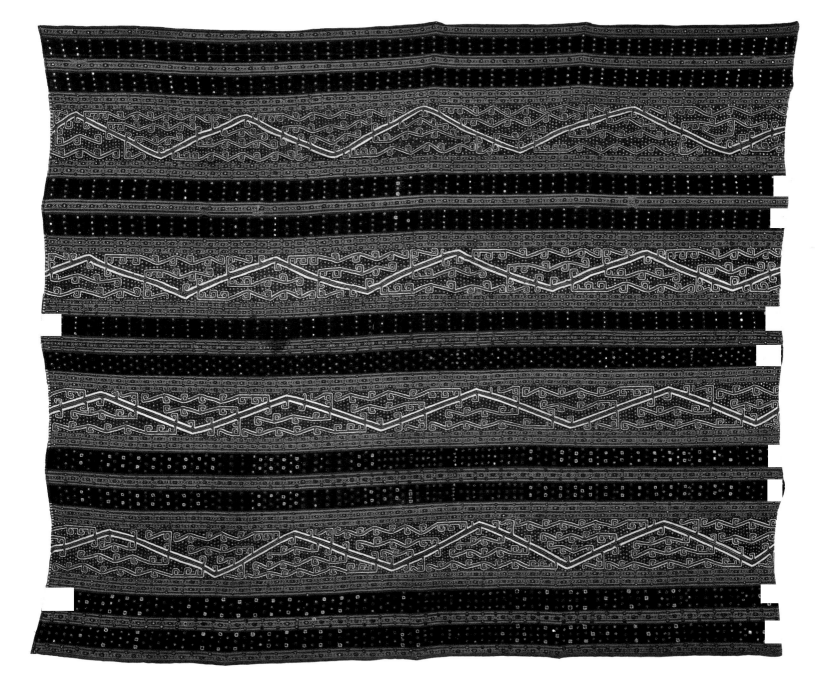

Palepai, Sumatra

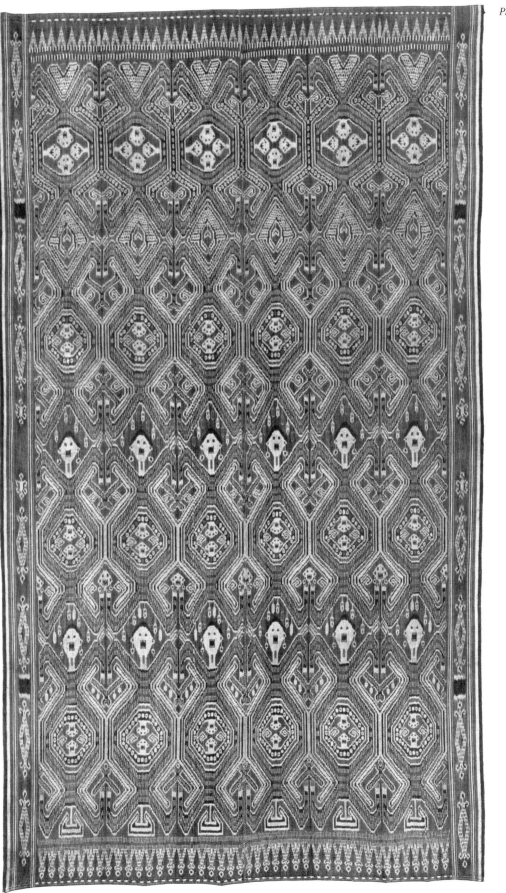

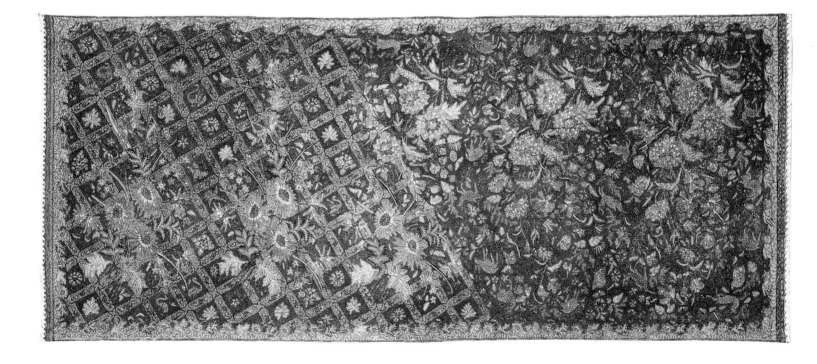

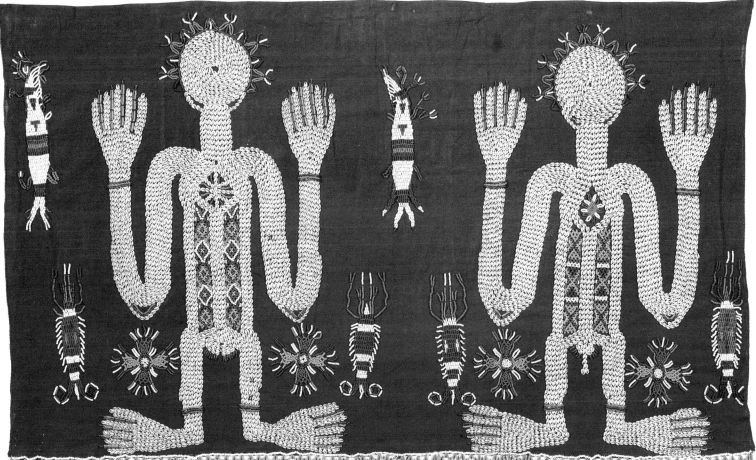

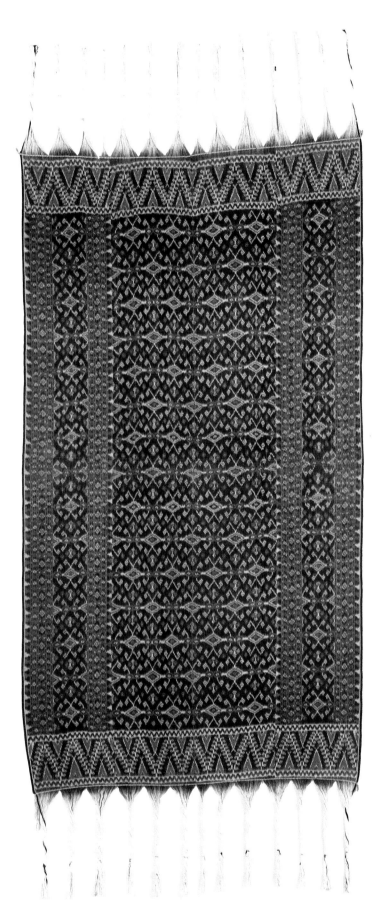

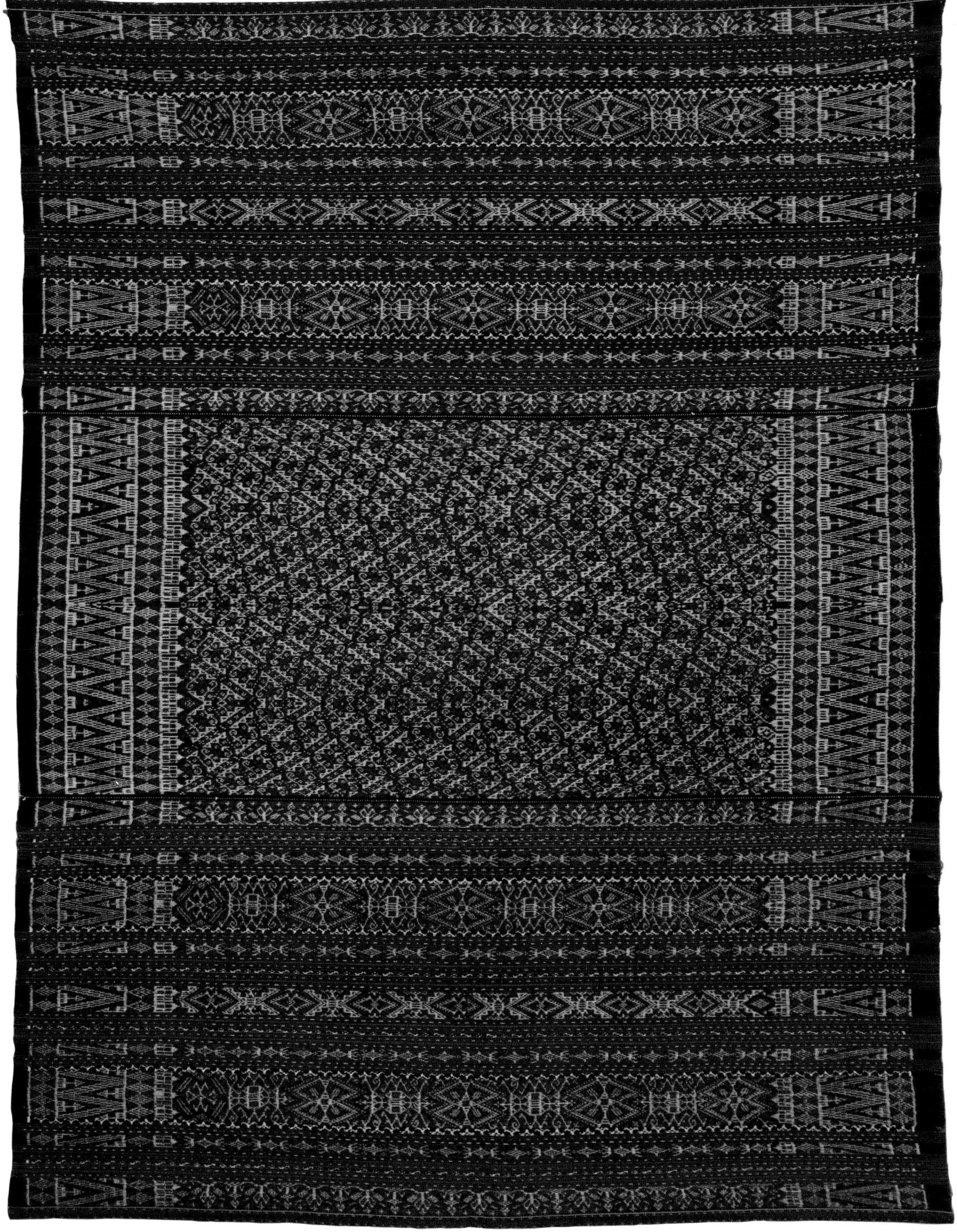

53
Sarong, Flores

Dr. Mattiebelle Gittinger

The variety of textiles woven on Sumatra is startling: simple plaids and complex woven scenes, glowing silks and somber cotton. Such diversity comes from an amalgam of factors and paramount among these has been Sumatra's position astride the trade routes of Southeast Asia. For over a millennium foreigners have not only introduced new textiles, which have influenced local traditions, but through their purchase of pepper, resins, ivory, and the like they have generated wealth that has permitted import of exotic materials. Metallic yarns, silk, artificial dyes, beads, and mirrored metals all came from foreign sources. Accumulation of wealth also fostered the manufacture and sale of textiles instead of the more conservative practice of weaving only for personal or family use. This was certainly a factor in the development of the opulent gold and silver cloth normally associated with this island.

There were, however, ethnic groups in the interior of Sumatra that remained remote from these contacts and until recently resisted innovations in their traditional weaving. The Batak are one of these groups. Surrounded by the mountain peaks of north central Sumatra they still have a flourishing weaving craft relatively unaffected by foreign contact. Their textiles are more clearly associated with social and religious customs than those made today on the coast, where such customs are now distorted or nonexistent.

The majority of the Batak cloths are large plain weave cotton fabrics in somber blue or rust relieved by muted stripes, simple warp ikat patterns (see no. 1), and finely twined weft borders. Called by the generic term *ulos,* these textiles are woven by the Toba Batak to be worn over the shoulder or around the hips in the manner of a sarong. An exceptional type termed *ragidup* (see no. 2) has white end panels with precisely woven geometric designs worked in black or red supplementary weft yarns. The Angkola Batak specialize in quite a different textile (see no. 3), now imitated by many neighboring groups, which has brightly colored designs of diamonds, eight-pointed stars, variations of simple geometric forms, and many accents of beads inserted in the weaving process. Occasionally the weaver even wishes the wearer well with some trimly worked slogan. The techniques used in the decorative elements are supplementary wefts and tapestry weave which are often interspersed with bands of twill weave.

The designs have meanings within the tribal context although fewer and fewer Batak understand them. Most widely known is the significance of the large topmost row of designs in the white end panels of the *ragidup* (see no. 2). The characteristics of these designs determine if the panel is male or female, and each cloth contains both types. The designs of the female panel, however, are more important, for these are "read" by a knowledgeable person when this cloth is made to be given to a daughter pregnant with her first child. It is the daughter's *ulos ni tondi,* or "soul cloth," and the designs encode her future.[1]

The Batak attribute a supportive quality to all of their textiles. A mother might give her son a cloth when he goes on a journey abroad as a source of protection against the unknown. Elderly persons when ill might seek the comfort of a particular cloth. However, it is in the prescribed giving of textiles sanctioned by the customary laws that this almost mystical quality is most clearly seen.

The two patrilineages that become associated by a marriage exist in an unevenly balanced alliance in which the bride-givers, called *hula-hula,* are superior to the bride-takers, called *anak boru.* They are linked by a tightly structured system of reciprocal gift exchange in which all the gifts coming from the bride-givers carry the term *ulos* ("cloth") and those from the bride-takers, *piso* ("knife"). The latter term is used only in a categorical sense in that knives, considered masculine, are not given, but rather other "masculine" goods such as money, carabao, or pigs. In contrast, the *ulos* designation, while it always has included other items, still demands the actual transfer of traditional woven cloth.[2] It is with these gifts that the superior bride-givers strengthen the vital force, or *sahala,* of the bride-takers. These exchanges draw upon the resources of many people within each lineage and are major components of ceremonies accompanying marriage, birth, death, and other life-crisis periods. As many as 275 cloths are known to have been given in one wedding exchange and 70 or more would not be unusual at the funeral of an elderly person.[3]

On such occasions certain textiles are more appropriate than others. For instance, the bride's father wraps the groom's mother in a prestigious *ragidup* during the wedding ceremony, but envelopes the young bride and groom in a slightly less venerable cloth more suited to their age. Maternal grandparents would give a newborn grandchild a still less prestigious cloth, such as a *suri-suri* (see no. 1). However, the *hula-hula* would never give the *suri-suri* or the more commonly seen child's carrying cloth, the *ulos mangiring,* at the funeral of a child because this would bring misfortune on all children yet to be born to that family. Thus there are categories among the *ulos* that determine their role in the cycle of gift exchange.

Along the coasts of Sumatra most of the ancient Indonesian traditions still observed by the Batak have been changed or may possibly never have existed. This is particularly true on the east and north coasts, where a synthesis of the Malay, Javanese, Chinese, Arabic, and Indian cultures now prevails. Also, the people of these areas, as well as of the western Menangkabau region, long ago embraced Islam and it is not clear how this affected preexisting textile traditions. Whether or not at the expense of tradition, it was an amalgamation of these influences that gave rise to the sumptuous silk and gold textiles for which Sumatra is renowned. Sericulture was introduced, probably by Chinese traders, and in certain areas, such as the north coast, thrived to such an extent that at one time silk was exported.[4] Turkey red dyeing, lac dyeing, and complex vegetable dyeing were also popular in the coastal areas.[5] Metallic yarns and techniques such as weft ikat, *plangi, tritik,* embroidery, and even batik added to the decorative possibilities available to local weavers. Also, commerce promoted the rise of moneyed aristocrats who sought out exotic foreign textiles and even imported foreign weavers.

These factors all coalesced into what may be termed a coastal silk cloth tradition, even though the phenomenon also exists in some inland areas. In general it is characterized by geometric or small floral designs, weft rather than warp ikat, designs featuring frames or borders, and highly ornamental details. Many of these features trace directly to the prestigious Indian *patola* textiles, which were traded to Southeast Asia beginning in the sixteenth century or before.[6] However, Sumatran weavers assimilated the major features of these exotic cloths and recast them in a local style.

Palembang on the east coast is particularly famous for textiles of this tradition. The weavers here, even today, produce glowing red silks adorned with gentle yellow, green, and blue ikat designs (see no. 6) that are complemented by splendid overlay patterns in supplementary gold or silver weft yarns. Traditionally woven as sarongs, *kain,* shoulder cloths, and head wrappers, these cloths today are used largely for religious holidays and weddings. The bride and groom in particular are bedecked with gold *kain* and shoulder cloths cinched at the waist with an ornate belt. Glittering gold crowns and bracelets help to complete the regal effect of their costumes.

It is uncertain whether such textiles were ever a major element of dress in the coastal areas. They were, however, important symbols of wealth and prestige, and the custom arose for wealthy families to display their costly hoards of textiles with an ornamented ceremonial bed. The heavily embroidered trappings of the bed are in themselves considered treasures. Precious cloths are hung on a frame near the bed, as in Bengkulen,[7] or on a special rack over the bed in Indrigiri.[8] This tableau, which may be seen in homes along the east, north, and west coasts, is set up in an inner room primarily at wedding celebrations, but may be seen on other life-crisis occasions as well.

Use of these costly textiles does not seem to be governed by the time-sanctioned rules of gift exchanges that exist between Batak bride-givers and bride-takers. It seems, although textile exchanges in the coastal areas are not well documented, that rather than being classified as "female" goods, these locally made textiles represent wealth alone. This is not an illogical evolution when textiles cease to be woven by family members and become purchased goods. Thus the Palembang custom of the groom's supplying the bride with at least three types of cloth, including the gold and silk wedding garb,[9] reverses the traditional flow of textile goods in Indonesian exchanges and becomes instead a display of the groom's wealth. The bride does later give the groom an ikat textile and this may be a remnant of earlier gift exchange patterns.

A more traditional flow of textiles is found among some groups of the highland Menangkabau, where the bride gives the groom a gold woven textile and an imported cloth. In this matrilocal society the cloths symbolize the groom's welcome into the bride's home. However, if the marriage dissolves before there are children, the *kain* must be returned.[10] Elsewhere among the Menangkabau the groom and his female relatives present textiles to the bride and her family and then receive the two symbolic *kain* at a later ceremony.[11]

The indigenous term for supplementary weft, *songket,* gives silk and gold textiles their name and one speaks of them as *kain songket.* Designs worked in this technique, used either in borders or in center fields, are star and rosette forms which carry the names of various flowers, vines, fruits, the sun, stars, and the like.[12] Also, the *tumpal* at the ends of the cloth are made either by supplementary weft yarns or by a weft ikat. This border of triangles, locally termed *puncak rebung* ("bamboo shoot"), is a traditional Indonesian design found elsewhere on sarongs and *slendang.* In the *songket* border adjoining the *tumpal* are often either small *naga* or bird forms or, less frequently, a winged creature possibly taken from Western heraldry. Foreign influences such as rose and arabesque forms appear in the ikat designs as well as *naga* and frontal bird motifs. Certainly some of these elements derive from Javanese batik.

Plangi and *tritik* were additional techniques used to pattern silk, and the finest of these were also made in Palembang. Their designs and format are closely related to Indian *plangi* textiles, which also seem to have inspired the brighter and more varied range of dyes used on these cloths. These techniques are most commonly associated with shoulder cloths, belts, and wrappers worn over the breast. They were made by superimposing several layers of imported fabric and tying the layers simultaneously, thus producing several identical cloths.[13]

Today the materials for these cloths are all imported, including synthetic dyes which give the current cloths a somewhat more strident tone. The metallic yarns, while never of pure gold, are now a base alloy considered distinctly inferior by Palembang weavers to the yarns once imported from China, India, and Europe. The best cloths being woven today utilize metallic yarns unraveled from old garments.

Foreign contacts also introduced embroidery to Sumatra and it is practiced throughout the island on such items as jackets, bed hangings, pillows, food covers, and wedding garments. Most of these, however, are heavily indebted to Chinese and European sources. Only the women of Lampong, the southernmost district in Sumatra, were able to assimilate this technique of embroidery and recast it in truly indigenous expressions. They did this in decorating their heavy cotton sarongs, called *tapis,* which then became glittering accouterments to their lavish ceremonial occasions. The *tapis* begins as a large rectangle composed of two locally woven cotton panels sewn together at the selvage. It is then embroidered and, when complete, the whole is sewn into a tube and worn like a sarong. In some examples, however, the embroidery was done on separate cotton strips and then attached. *Tapis* are no longer made in most of Lampong but as recently as 1971 a few of the Abung people in the east were still producing particularly ostentatious cloths whose surfaces were almost entirely covered with gold yarn. These metallic yarns are couched onto locally woven cotton cloth striped in brown, blue black, or deep yellow. The couching stitches that hold the metal yarns are arranged in geometric patterns that produce pleasing rhythms across the gold surface. Most *tapis* are skillfully planned so the forms created in the gold yarns interact with and are complemented by the muted tones and variable widths of the background stripes.

Small mirror pieces called *cermuk* were also embroidered onto the *tapis* surface and the Kauer people on the west coast preferred this embellishment to all others.[14] They used them on their *tapis,* often in combination with silk embroidery, and to a lesser extent on jackets. The *cermuk,* small square pieces of mirrored metal cut from larger imported sheets,[15] are held in place by embroidery, which also rounds off the corners. Whether the *cermuk* were aligned in ordered rows, grouped in simple geometric conformations, or casually scattered across the surface of the cloth, their quantity was most important to the Kauer. Some cloths took over a year to make and there are examples of *tapis* weighing more than ten pounds. A *tapis* and jacket constituted the festival dress of young single women, who were required to make these garments before marriage. A suitor's inquiries often took the form of asking if the *tapis* were finished.[16]

A remarkably different type of *tapis* was made in the mountainous interior region. Here they were made with large bands of complex embroidered designs alternating with either areas of warp ikat (see no. 5) or plain bands of contrasting brown and yellow stripes. Both the motifs and the style of the embroidered bands are unusual. Curving organic shapes emerge as ships carrying trees, people, and small houses. These sprout tendrils that fill the band with a welter of sinuous forms sprinkled with *cermuk.* In other examples the shapes are beyond recognition, having dissolved into amoebalike insubstantiality. The figures are worked in a satin stitch of one color, then outlined in a contrasting color. This outlining of the forms accentuates their curvilinear quality and has prompted speculation that the designs originated in painting on wood, bamboo, or metal.

This is also suggested by the use of the plain stitch to fill all available background areas, which gives a three-dimensional effect to the design surface.[17] The designs are embroidered in gentle tones of cream white, blue, and reddish brown silk on a dark indigo blue cotton ground and provide a marked contrast to the angular rhombs and diamond patterns of the bordering brown cotton ikat bands.

The ship and tree designs on these embroidered bands have been compared in style and content to paintings made by the Dayak of Borneo.[18] These paintings on elongated wooden planks were hung before the house of a dead person and later used in the funeral ceremony. They, too, show ships and trees and many other details that recall the Lampong cloths. This coincidence has led one authority to interpret the scenes on the *tapis* as ships-of-the-dead,[19] but ship symbolism exists elsewhere in Sumatra and has a broader significance.

The most remarkable renderings of ships occur in a type of ceremonial textile once woven along the south coast of Sumatra. These cloths are marvels of the weaver's art, delighting the eye with designs of ships, men, animals, trees, birds, and small buildings. Because of the predominant use of the ship motif they are called "ship cloths" in the West or sometimes "Krui" or "Kroe cloths," after the small coastal villages where early twentieth-century vendors said they originally acquired the textiles.

In Sumatra these textiles have other names that differentiate three basic types. One is the *palepai* ("ship") or *sesaibalak* ("big wall"), which is an exceptionally long and narrow textile often exceeding three meters in length (see nos. 7,8). A second form, called *tatibin,* is also narrow, but rarely exceeds one meter (see nos. 9,10). The third type has a virtually square format that is less than a meter on a side; these have the name *tampan* (see nos. 11-13).[20]

All share similar technical details. Colored supplementary wefts are used to form the designs on a plain weave foundation. In the long cloths these wefts tend to be discontinuous while both continuous and discontinuous supplementary wefts occur on the *tampan.* The fibers, which are cotton or occasionally a lightly spun silk, are dyed rich yellow, reddish brown, or blue black. A natural unbleached cotton is always used in the foundation. In the *palepai* and *tatibin,* metallic yarns may appear in the weaving and thin metallic strips are frequently tacked to the surface of the cloth by bast fibers. In the best examples these elements were judiciously combined to produce some of the finest textiles made in Indonesia. In apparently later textiles, harsh dyes and excessive use of the metallic yarns result in cloths of far less charm.

The *tampan* are the most numerous of the ship cloths and at one time were probably woven throughout much of South Sumatra. Today a few of the small cloths exist along the south and west coasts and occasionally still function in a ritual capacity. Considerably less common are the *palepai* and *tatibin* which, according to examples remaining in 1971, were woven only along the south coast of Sumatra. These, too, were ceremonial accouterments, but so many have appeared on Western markets in the past five years that it is doubtful any significant number remain in use in Sumatra today.

The *tampan* seem to have evolved into the Indonesian symbolic textile par excellence. Not only were large numbers included in the bride's dowry,[21] but even today they enter into gift exchanges similar to those found among the Batak. These squares wrapped around small gifts of food are exchanged between the lineages of a man and wife. However, unlike the Batak system, the flow of these gifts occurs almost reciprocally, at one time placing the burden on the man's lineage, at another on the woman's. These exchanges originally occurred at all life-crisis ceremonies involving the same participants who had initially been linked by *tampan* exchanges at the time of marriage. In recent years the cloths have only been nominally given in these ceremonies, later being returned to the owner. This may be a contemporary response to their scarcity or may have been the custom even when they were still being woven. In any case, the exchange of these cloths continues to identify and enumerate the multiple bonds between lineages joined by marriage.[22]

Tampan once served other functions in which they assumed symbolic significance of a more varied nature. In examining some of these occasions it appears the *tampan* identified the nexus of ritual concern and by their very presence delineated a ritual sphere. Thus even today in some areas the bride sits on one or more of the small cloths during specific times in the wedding ceremony. The elder who presided over yearly law gatherings sat on a *tampan,* and on other ceremonial occasions certain groups of elders gathered around a large *tampan* to eat the festival meal. In the south the handles of the funeral bier were wrapped with *tampan,* and on the Krui coast the head of a deceased person rested on one of the small cloths while the body was washed. The *tampan* even entered house-consecration ceremonies, for one was tied to the ridge pole during the ritual and it stayed there for the life of the house. Without doubt these textiles became ritual markers, serving to differentiate ceremonial occasions from everyday routine.

The design elements on these small cloths are varied both in the number of forms and the style in which they are rendered. In certain compositions ships carrying trees, shrines, and people fill an entire cloth (see no. 12), while in others a simple geometric shape is repeated in narrow studied rows. Still other compositions are so literal they seem to be a graphic rendering of a story or myth that just eludes our understanding. In this last type the style of the figures frequently recalls the *wayang*

shadow puppets of Java and certainly strong influences did cross the Straits of Sunda to affect the textiles. The size rather than the designs of the *tampan* seems to have been most important in determining their functions. Styles in composition or weaving can seldom be assigned to specific regions, although the *wayang* influenced figures are found only along the south coasts.

Tampan could be made and used by all levels of society, but this was not true of the *palepai* and *tatibin*. Only the senior representatives of the patrilineal descent groups who carried the title *penyimbang suku* and *penyimbang marga* had the right to use the long cloths. They could, however, grant others the right to use the cloths. As the system of ranks and titles proliferated along the south coast it is probable that siblings or others gained access to these rights and had textiles made for their own use. Even so, their use was essentially restricted to an aristocratic layer of society.

In ceremonies the *palepai* was hung on the right wall in the inner room of the house, where it acted as the backdrop to the principal person. In marriage rituals this was traditionally the bride, although more recently the groom has joined her before the *palepai* at specific times. When the bride first returns to her house after the wedding ceremony, the occasion may be marked with a celebration in which her parents hang one of the long cloths. Shortly after they were born, first children were presented at the maternal grandparent's home in a setting before the *palepai* to receive a name. This was also the scene for the festivities surrounding a boy's circumcision. At one time the textiles were also hung when a man advanced in social rank and at funerals.

The *palepai* formed part of a tableau encompassing other objects which, in some southern areas, included the *tatibin*. Details of these scenes varied, but generally included a pile of several small, thin mattresslike cushions and a group of hard bolsters arranged in a couch form that served as the seat in front of the *palepai*. This was lined with *tampan* and the mattress pile was covered with a *tatibin*. Another *tatibin* was wrapped around a wooden box set to the right of the bride's seat. Such boxes, now rarely seen, were part of the heirlooms of a lineage and during the ceremony held piles of festival cloths and jewelry.

During the life-crisis ceremonies other *palepai* were hung to the right and left of the major textile. These belonged to other men of rank who existed in a rigidly prescribed relationship to the owner of the centrally placed *palepai*. These men were positioned to the right or left of the principal, and the order in which their textiles were hung reflected this arrangement. In certain rare cases an entire room might be hung with *palepai,* with each placed according to the hereditary position of the owner. Obviously these long cloths are symbolic systems that convey a range of meanings. In their ceremonial context they accurately portray the social position of the owner and the relationship of his lineage to the larger association of lineages, the *marga*.

The designs of the *palepai* were an integral part of this symbolic system, but the precise details of how they functioned are not clear. There are, however, four distinct classes of *palepai* designs, and each has at least one unique characteristic.[23] A single large blue ship with projecting trifurcated bow and stern is the unique feature of one class (see no. 7). A red ship with abruptly rising bow and stern characterizes a second. Most frequently the red ships appear in pairs on a single cloth (see no. 8), although some textiles have only a single red ship; these may constitute a distinct category. The third class of *palepai* has at least two rows of stylized human forms in which each figure seems to wear a horned head-gear. (Similar figures can be seen in the *tatibin* no. 10.) The fourth class of *palepai* is characterized by the organization of designs into four or more discrete panels that may be a continuous woven textile or several segments sewn together. It is probable that at one time these four or possibly five distinct types of *palepai* represented the four lineages, or *suku,* that originally constituted the larger association, or *marga.* When hung according to the relationships of the lineages they would have mirrored the internal structure of the *marga* as a whole.

Ship and tree assemblages and animals carrying riders are the major motifs of the *palepai.* As images suggesting transition, they are appropriate designs for textiles used in naming, circumcision, marriage, and death ceremonies that celebrate transitions to new stages of existence. The people of South Sumatra utilized the ship conformation as a major structuring principle, and it appears as the basic conceptual form for houses and ceremonial processions. Earlier literature[24] has tended to label the motif as "ships-of-the-dead," but it is evident, as others have also noted, that the designs have a greater significance than transition to death alone.[25] They are highly evolved symbolic systems and, by the way they are hung in all life-crisis ceremonies, portray the society's structure of rank and authority.

The history of these ship cloths is enigmatic. The reasons for both their original use and their demise remain conjectural. The skill needed to produce these remarkable textiles is now completely lost and apparently has been for three-quarters of a century. Supposition of why this happened centers on a combination of factors, including the abolition of slavery in 1859, the decline of the pepper trade, and changing marriage traditions.[26] However, while they flourished, the cloths represented a peak in the textile art of Indonesia.

A Batak family poses for a studio photograph sometime prior to 1920. The costumes are somber in color with dark blues, blacks, and white. Each person has an ulos suri suri *over his shoulder similar to the one shown in no. 1.*

Notes

1.
Vergouwen, p. 100, and Gittinger, 1975, pp. 19ff.

2.
Vergouwen, pp. 58-63.

3.
Gittinger, 1975, p. 24.

4.
Veltman, p. 18.

5.
Ibid., pp. 73-74, and Bühler, 1941.

6.
Bühler, 1959, pp. 1-2.

7.
Gittinger, unpublished field notes, 1971.

8.
Obdeyn, p. 109.

9.
Communication of R. H. M. Akib, Palembang, 1975.

10.
Toorn, p. 213.

11.
Ibid., pp. 216-17.

12.
Jasper and Pirngadie, p. 239.

13.
Nabholz-Kartaschoff, p. 20, and Bühler, 1954, p. 3727.

14.
The distribution of *tapis* styles is based on examples remaining in Sumatra in these regions in 1971.

15.
Hille, p. 179.

16.
Gittinger, unpublished field notes, 1971.

17.
Alfred Steinmann, "The Ship of the Dead in the Textile Art of Indonesia," *Ciba Review,* vol. 52, September 1946, p. 1891.

18.
Ibid., p. 1889.

19.
Ibid., p. 1890.

20.
Gittinger, 1972.

21.
op't Land, p. 114.

22.
Gittinger, 1972, pp. 21-29, and 1976, pp. 211-14,

23.
Ibid., pp. 220-21.

24.
Steinmann, "Ship of the Dead."

25.
Palm, p. 68.

26.
op't Land, p. 115.

1

Ulos Suri-Suri (symbolic cloth)
North Sumatra (Batak)
Warp ikat on warp-faced plain
weave, twining
Cotton
Warp: 198.1 cm.; weft: 70.5 cm.
Los Angeles County Museum of Art
Costume Council Fund
M.74.17

The Batak never expanded their ikat patterns to include recognizable figures, always using only simple geometric forms. Nevertheless, by their placement of designs, their distinctive use of thin stripes and small flecks, their decorative borders, and their variations in dyes, they produced an entire range of textiles with unique characteristics. Differences between the cloths may seem minor to the casual observer, but they are quite important to the Batak and affect the use of the cloth. For example, the thin stripes and the three large zones of ikat of this piece are critical to its identity as a *ulos suri-suri*, a cloth appropriately given on the birth of a child.

2

Ragidup (symbolic cloth)
North Sumatra (Batak)
Plain weave, supplementary weft on
warp-faced plain weave
Cotton
Warp: 242 cm.; weft: 127 cm.
Los Angeles County Museum of Art
Costume Council Fund
M.74.18.6

The most prestigious of the Batak
textiles, the *ragidup* is also the most
complex. The white end panels of
the central zone are interlocked
with the striped center field by
superimposing the white warp
yarns over the warp of the center
field and inserting a few weft yarns
to lock the new warp in place. The
dark warps are then cut away and
weaving continues on the white
yarns. The reason why these white
panels were not woven separately
and then sewn into place, as the
two dark side panels were, may lie
in the symbolic qualities of the
cloth.[1]

1.
Gittinger, 1975, p. 26.

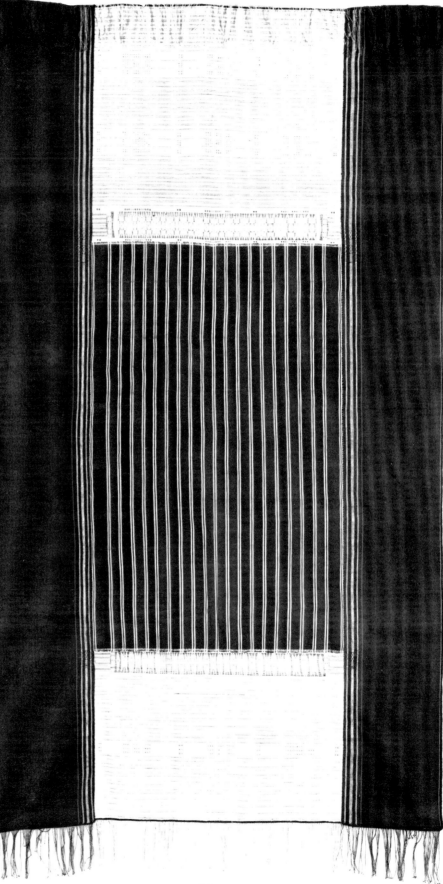

3

Ulos Godang (skirt cloth)
North Sumatra (Angkola Batak)
Supplementary weft, warp-faced plain
weave, twill, twining, tapestry
wrapping
Cotton, wool, beads
Warp: 208.3 cm.; weft: 87.6 cm.
Los Angeles County Museum of Art
Costume Council Fund
M.74.18.8

4

Tapis (skirt cloth)
Lampong, South Sumatra
Embroidery on warp-faced plain weave
Cotton, silk, mirror fragments
Warp: 127.6 cm.; weft: 109.8 cm.
Los Angeles County Museum of Art
Costume Council Fund
M.73.73.4
(See color plate, p. 13)

Although culturally similar to other Batak groups, the Angkola Batak weave a strikingly dissimilar textile, the *ulos godang.* It depends on various types of weaving—including a tapestry wrapping of grouped warp yarns, twill, and the addition of beads—rather than ikat alone for its decoration. The beads are inserted in the body of the cloth during the weaving process, but the borders are laced into position with the aid of a subsidiary frame after the cloth is removed from the loom. The *ulos godang* is highly valued by all the Batak and frequently imitated by other Batak groups. This cloth is worn in the manner of a sarong, and a similar but narrower textile woven by the Angkola, called a *parompa sadum,* serves as a baby carrier.

In a few regions of South Sumatra makers of the women's *tapis* shifted their focus from narrow bands of embroidery to the task of embroidering increasing numbers of mirror pieces onto the surface of the cloth. Eventually *tapis* patterns were named for the amount and arrangement of the glittering squares while the embroidered bands dwindled into modest scrolls and simple lines. The flamboyance of the mirrors was offset by the broad stripes in muted browns and yellows of the underlying traditional *tapis* cloth, and the resulting juxtaposition of old and new elements produced a richly decorative effect.

Tapis (skirt cloth)
Lampong, South Sumatra
Warp ikat and embroidery on warp-faced plain weave
Cotton, silk
Warp: 119.4 cm.; weft: 114.3 cm.
Professor Samuel Eilenberg

This woman's skirt cloth made in the mountainous interior of the Lampong region juxtaposes two quite different styles: angular geometric forms in the ikat panels and sinuous organic shapes in the embroidered bands. This dichotomy of style may have arisen because the ikat designs originated in a weaving tradition practiced by women, while the embroidered designs stemmed from a masculine source. By custom, suitors presented their girlfriends with designs to be embroidered on the *tapis*,[1] and it seems logical they would have taken these from a design inventory most familiar to them, such as painting or wood carving.

1.
Jasper and Pirngadie, 1912, p. 303.

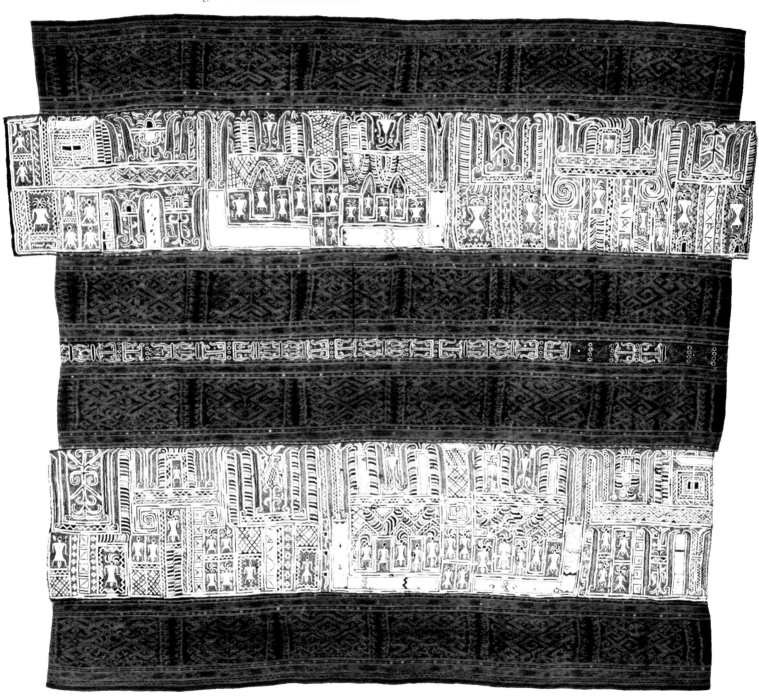

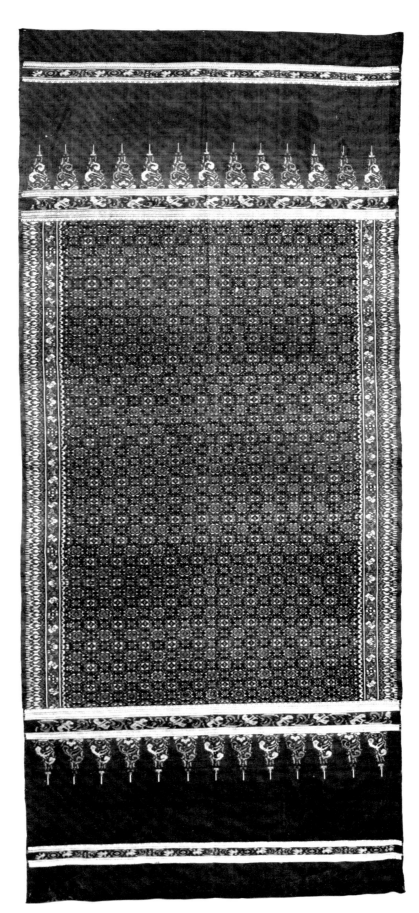

6

Slendang (shoulder cloth)
Palembang, Sumatra
Weft ikat on weft-faced plain weave
Silk
Warp: 227.3 cm.; weft: 121.9 cm.
Los Angeles County Museum of Art
Costume Council Fund
M.74.18.9

The small, precise weft ikat patterning in the center field of this shoulder cloth as well as the restrained *tumpal* elements in the end zones makes this a subtly intricate cloth. The fact that it shares many qualities, including the composition and the flamelike motif of the lateral borders, with weft ikats made on mainland Southeast Asia recalls their common heritage in the Hindu textiles that were traded throughout the area. It may also indicate that textiles woven on the Southeast Asia mainland and in parts of Sumatra were traded directly between these areas and further influenced the similar development of their textiles. Until the fourteenth century Palembang was the center of Indonesia's largest empire and controlled much of the trade through the sea lanes of Southeast Asia. It is natural to assume that even at this early date textiles from many sources were exerting influences on the traditions of coastal Sumatra.

7

Palepai (ceremonial cloth)
South Sumatra
Supplementary weft on plain weave
Cotton, silk
Warp: 284.4 cm.; weft: 62.2 cm.
Los Angeles County Museum of Art
Costume Council Fund
M.73.73.5
(See color plate, p. 14)

Palepai featuring a single blue ship frequently also include house forms with curves emerging from the sides. Because the traditional houses of the interior mountain regions had decorative projections, it is probable that the houses of this textile are schematic representations of such dwellings. The blue ship compositions thus seem to represent an earthly realm, as opposed to the sacred sphere of the red ship *palepai.* These complementary themes suggest that there was a highly evolved ordering and significance among the four or five major types of *palepai,* which at one time probably mirrored a social structure.[1]

1.
Gittinger, 1976.

8

Palepai (ceremonial cloth), detail
South Sumatra
Supplementary weft on plain weave
Cotton, silk
Warp: 350.5 cm.; weft: 70 cm.
Los Angeles County Museum of Art
Costume Council and Museum
Associates Purchase
M.77.107
(See cover)

Palepai with two red ships are not unusual, but the multiple compositions of this textile are rarely found in the long cloths. This breach of convention—as well as the large size of the human figures, which are customarily small in relation to the entire scene—suggests the cloth was woven relatively late. The exaggerated profile of the figures with straight shoulders and stylized costumes shows influences from the Javanese shadow play.

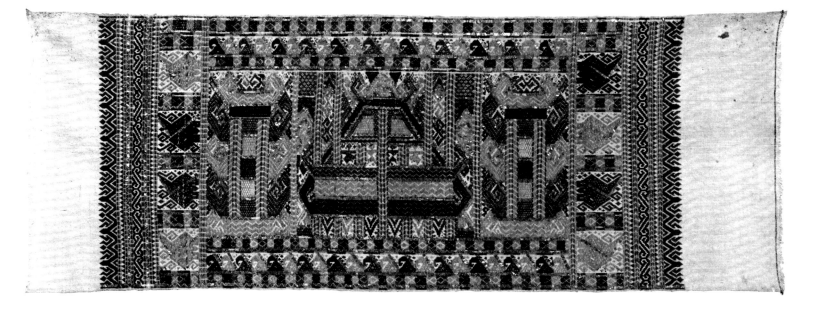

9

Tatibin (ceremonial cloth)
South Sumatra
Supplementary weft on plain weave
Cotton, silk
Warp: 100 cm.; weft: 36 cm.
Los Angeles County Museum of Art
Costume Council Fund
M.77.81.17
(See illustration, opposite)

10

Tatibin (ceremonial cloth)
South Sumatra
Supplementary weft on plain weave
Cotton, silk
Warp: 109 cm.; weft: 40 cm.
Los Angeles County Museum of Art
Costume Council Fund
M.77.81.19
(See illustration, below)

Tatibin designs are almost always similar to those of the *palepai,* merely reducing in scale a few select elements found on the long cloths. For example, the figure in no. 10 appears in one class of *palepai,* where it is repeated in two or more long horizontal rows. Wherever it is used, the figure remains enigmatic, always with the same perplexing stylization and only the horn or ship-shaped head decoration to suggest an interpretation. This may be the huge, glittering arched headgear, the *siger,* worn by unmarried girls and brides. In other *tatibin* the design elements borrowed from the *palepai* are abstracted into squared and angular shapes (see no. 9) that cover the cloth surface like the pieces of a puzzle. Only on close inspection do the forms emerge as flags, banners, houses, and birds. *Tatibin* are the least numerous of the ship cloths in Western collections and are frequently mislabeled as *tampan.*

11

Tampan (ceremonial cloth)
South Sumatra
Supplementary weft on plain weave
Cotton
Warp: 62.9 cm.; weft: 61 cm.
Los Angeles County Museum of Art
Costume Council Fund
M.73.73.8

Specific *tampan* compositions were repeated dozens of times by various weavers, and as the repetition continued, forms changed subtly and the identity of particular elements seems to have been lost. With the aid of other examples we know that this composition essentially represents two birds flanking a small building, but here the building has gained armlike appendages and the birds strangely distorted heads. The inverted boat at the top of the composition is a common design element found in many *tampan* compositions.

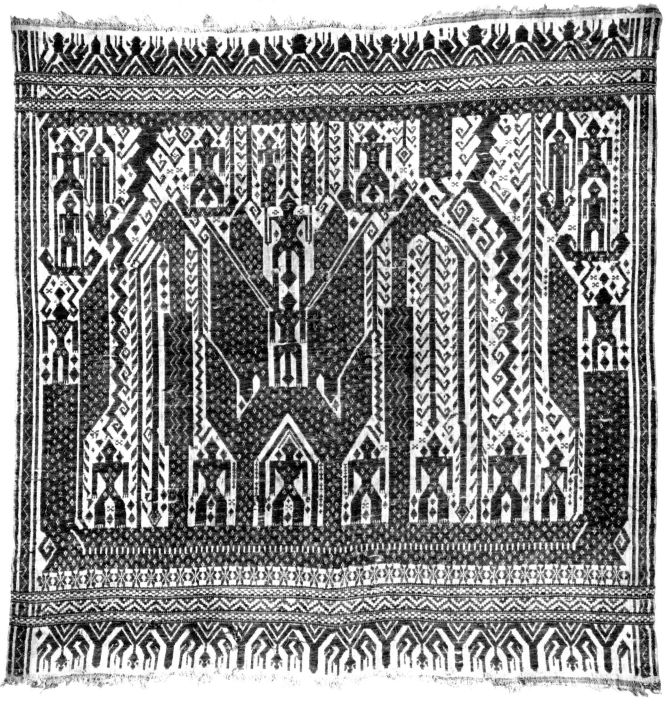

12
Tampan (ceremonial cloth)
South Sumatra
Supplementary weft on plain weave
Cotton
Warp: 66 cm.; weft: 56.5 cm.
Los Angeles County Museum of Art
Costume Council Fund
M.77.81.4

This *tampan* composition is extremely puzzling for it seems to represent a myth or narrative. A ship carries a large house that encompasses a smaller house and umbrella shapes that shelter human figures. Additional umbrella forms and human figures surround the house and all is engulfed in a welter of bird forms. We can only surmise that the umbrella shapes recall the ancestor shrines from South Sumatra and that the composition deals with the commemoration of ancestors.

13

Tampan (ceremonial cloth)
South Sumatra
Supplementary weft on plain weave,
metallic strips
Cotton
Warp: 43.8 cm.; weft: 42.5 cm.
Los Angeles County Museum of Art
Costume Council Fund
M.77.81.15

The metallic strips and discontinuous supplementary wefts on this *tampan* are more common technical features of the *palepai*. Their presence here suggests that this small cloth was woven along the south coast, where the long textiles were also made. Repetition of small design elements in horizontal rows is a commonly used device on *tampan* compositions, as are the multiple tiers of decorative bands used to frame the central design field. *Tampan* compositions, however, are not usually this complex; the majority have simple geometric forms repeated within a bordered matrix. This simplicity is understandable when one considers the great numbers of these cloths that were required and the labor needed to produce them.

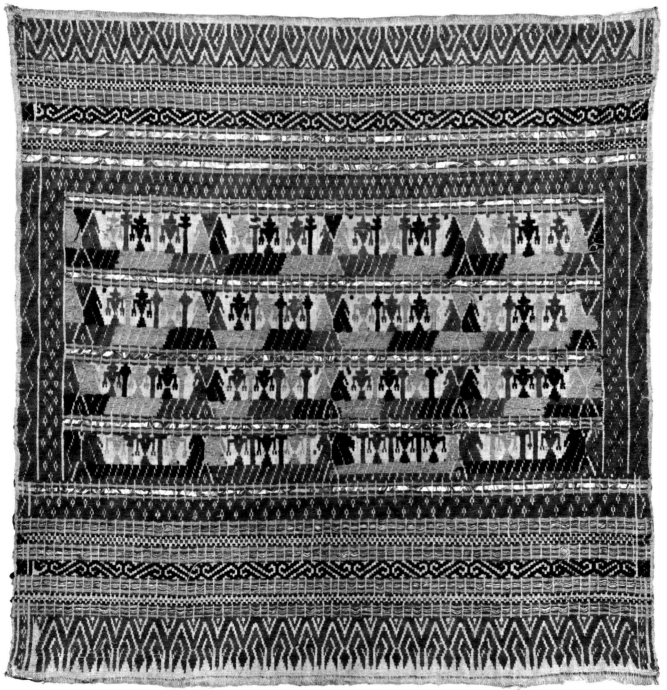

Anita Spertus and Jeff Holmgren

Borneo is the largest island in the Malay Archipelago and one of the most remote regions on earth. Interior communication is difficult and almost exclusively by river; only the coasts—inhabited by Malays and, during the early periods of Hindu colonization, by Indo-Javanese settlers—have been touched by the classical culture associated with Java, Sumatra, Malaya, and Bali. Inland Borneo is populated by diverse tribes, once subsumed under the designation Dayak (Malay, "native"), but now distinguished with specific local names. Though all of these groups possess ornamental traditions (beadwork, carving and painting, monumental wood sculpture, etc.) and many undertake simple weaving and plaiting, the magnificent ceremonial hangings and garments that give Borneo textiles eminence among Indonesian decorative arts are the work of only a few: the Ot Danum, Bahau, Apo Kayan, and, most importantly, the Iban.[1]

These inland tribes preserve and sustain in all their arts motifs and aesthetic principles from ancient central and east Asia (the original home-land of proto-Indonesian peoples) that are probably contemporaneous with their arrival millennia ago in the archipelago. Robert von Heine-Geldern[2] identifies the motifs of the initial neolithic phase of immigration (third and second millennia B.C.) as mainly representational. They relate to the sacral concerns of nature- and spirit-worship and include orant humans, animals, and plant forms of universal significance such as the tree of life. There are indications that these motifs, now more or less confined to eastern Indonesia, were once widespread in east Asia.[3]

A subsequent influence of great impact, which entered Indonesia with the Bronze Age during the first millennium B.C., ema-nated from the Dongson culture of Annam (central Vietnam), where Cham hill people speaking a Malayo-Polynesian language still live. This later style, mainly abstract and geometric, is particularly evident in the earliest extant textiles of the Iban tribe. Typical patterns are hooks emerg-ing from large geometric forms, spiral and S-shapes, and meanders, all elaborated and symmetrically combined with enormous variety.

Heine-Geldern identifies a third phase of design influence from the Late Chou period in China (ca. 770-222 B.C.), distinguished by a paramount concern with rhythm, to which the best Borneo craft owes "its remarkable freedom from symmetry, its phantastically stylized animal motifs, the delicacy of its lines, and its ability to combine a large number of varied patterns in one integrated and overall ornamental design."[4]

Often warlike, piratical, and fierce in resistance to external control, the tribes experienced no further significant contact with neighboring is-lands or foreign nations until the nineteenth century; their textiles exhibit no trace of the profound Indianization of design so evident in other Indonesian cultures.

Several techniques of Borneo textile decoration are represented here: ikat of the warp on cotton and bast fiber, supplementary warp and weft,

brocade, tapestry, embroidery, beadwork, and appliqué with objects such as coins, bells, and shells.[5] There are five main types of work, all produced by women.

Pua: Approximately blanket-size cotton ikats and *songkets* used as ceremonial hangings and as receptacles for carrying heads taken in war. Serving many ritual functions, they are considered efficacious in curing disease, are used to consecrate sacrifices, figure in the transfer of wealth, and are known to offer protection for mediums in a trance. They exhibit the widest design repertoire of all Bornean textiles. The term *pua* may derive etymologically from *ipoh,* a fig tree that once provided bark for clothing;[6] and although *pua* are the one class of weaving that in historical times has not served as apparel, this has probably not always been true.[7]

Bidang: Short, tubular women's skirts, usually decorated with cotton ikat or supplementary weft. Delicate in scale and meticulously dyed and woven, *bidang* are often particularly elegant and inventive in design.

Kalambi: Jackets worn by both men and women. They are executed with a virtuoso display of technique, frequently with figural designs (divining birds and ancestor figures predominate).

Sirat: Men's cotton loincloths, with attached panels at either end, usually of supplementary weft or tapestry work. *Sirat* are strips of narrow (about 18 inches) but long (15 or 16 feet) plain or warp-striped cotton wrapped about the waist and between the legs; the two small rectangular decorated panels hang in front and behind from the waist.

Dangdong: Men's cotton ceremonial shawls, used also to wrap offerings.

A formal structure of creators, divinities, and upper and lower worlds exists among the Iban but is mainly of concern to the shamans, bards, augurers, healers, and other specialists who communicate with the spirit world. In daily life, proper conduct toward deities, spirits, and the souls of the dead ensures the well-being of the harvest, the family, and the com-munity. Virtually every thing, whether inanimate (e.g., rocks and knives) or living, that is thought to affect the quality of Iban life possesses a spirit; sacrifice solicits their support, which can assure success in any en-deavor. The spirits' attitudes are revealed through omen birds and snakes, dreams, augury, and divining by inspection of pigs' livers. Deep significance is attached to the interpretation of such signs: a particular bird's flight from the wrong direction or an ominous deer bark often means that a war expedition or a farm in construction will be abandoned, however advanced the work may be. Spirits think and feel; they live in longhouses and engage in everyday activities; they relate to the living in a fully human manner.

Weaving was a sacred act. While engaged in tying, dyeing, and weav-ing, women withdrew from the community and abstained from sex and certain foods, trying to achieve identity with their physical and spiritual environment. Iban textiles embody a fantastic vegetable and animal world of growing, twirling, twisting shapes—a tangled world of shadow, of motion, of the unexpected. The Iban textile design system served tribal belief. Most of the designs represent spirited things, whose depiction by the weaver may imply her control, respect, knowledge or identification, and perhaps even communication. At one time certain designs were the exclusive property of particular weavers, and must have served not only as the emblem of the owner and her clan, but also as the expression of that clan's specific relation to the spirit world. Since designs had inherent value and could be purchased, their possession and accumulation indicated wealth.

Borneans, like other tribal Indonesians, have attached to designs inherited from ancient epochs a significance consonant with the current beliefs and ritual requirements of their particular group. The original meanings of these designs are no longer identifiable, if indeed they were ever conceptually founded. The most important motifs[8] are human (the spirit gods and the *antus,* souls of ancestors, whose representation, rarely found during the early period, was allowed only to wives or female relations of chiefs, successful warriors, and other highly respected men); crocodiles (a particularly sacred spirit, believed to be lord of the waters, a devourer of evil spirits); snakes (a feared creature, guardian of especially strong personalities); birds and deer (omen-bearers and intermediaries with the spirit world); rice and the areas prepared for its cultivation (the spirit of rice is perhaps the most deeply respected, every effort being made to avoid offending it or causing the plant physical harm); creeping vines, rattan, fruits, and flowers; and occasionally human heads.[9]

Some early motifs cataloged by Charles Hose[10] are mystifying, others mundane: "crossing back and forth along the river," "branches [of a tree] with fireflies," "bird pushing oar," "sleeping cats," "the wound caused by the sting of the wasp," "leeches swallowing one another," "fire-hearth without the earth for firing on," and so forth. In all these identifications caution is required, as there is no indication whether the name reported by Hose represented an authoritative tradition, a consensus among knowledgeable Iban, or an individual fancy. An apparently haphazard combination of these motifs within a single cloth compounds the uncertainty.

Whatever the meaning of the component designs, the visual impact of Iban textiles is unified: conceived as allover patterns blending abstract and stylized elements, the finest weavings differ from those of many other Indonesian regions by presenting an elegant net of intermingling movements rather than separate motifs disposed in hierarchical bands. Usually asymmetrical from top to bottom, occasionally so from side to side, they are always flowing and rhythmic. Perimeters of the individual designs frequently resolve in curled hooks that visually "grasp" the

ground of the cloth and convey a sense of energy in tension. Borders (once broad and glorious like those of the Toraja) became typically quick and slender, like the birds and serpents often captured in them. Ghostlike spirit faces and figures startle as they flicker into visibility in the net.

In the oldest cloths the pattern is spacious and noble in proportion. Homespun threads impart an active, tactile texture. Color has a distinctive deep resonance, the result of laboriously repeated dippings in the dye vat and dryings. By the 1880s the bands along the selvage sometimes have bright aniline stripes of commercially dyed thread, which supplement the basic organic dye inventory of red, blue, black, and (less commonly) brown, adding brilliance to the space they enclose. Beginning at the turn of the century factory-spun thread was used to produce entire textiles, and with its consistent and (until World War II) very high quality it permitted more careful, minute ikats. These threads, expensive and prestigious, generally occur on somewhat smaller, exceedingly precise *pua,* in which traditional patterns are preserved, though much reduced in size. Appearing from the earliest periods and produced in a distinct Iban district, the best of these little *pua* are flamboyant, innovative, and jewellike; but often the gracious breadth of earlier cloths gives way to an engineered intricacy. *Bidang,* with their smaller scale, are more consistently successful in the transition to imported materials.

In contrast to the various qualities of fine antique cloth—overall harmony, elaboration of borders with quick rhythm, deep organic colors, and powerful visual conceptions (the pulsing light of a tree with fireflies, the four colors in the sky at dawn, the frog who "hammers out children as they are born into the world")—the authority and sincerity of recent Iban weavings have been compromised by the modern era. With education, Christian proselytization, increased government intervention, and the irreconcilable example of Western material culture only a high-speed boat ride away, new motives and imagery have entered Iban textiles. Much cloth is now produced for commercial sale, with the result that cheap chemical dyes are increasingly favored while patterning is spare and perfunctory, consistent with the desire to produce in quantity with speed. Layout is hierarchical and often symmetrically banded, with borders composed of plain stripes or absent altogether. Images are literal, almost photographic. Increasingly we see rifles, bombs, riverboats, teapots; decapitated heads, formerly uncommon, now occur with marked frequency, perhaps as an exercise in nostalgia. The curvilinear quality of expert ikat, most difficult to achieve, yields to straight lines and boxed shapes. Mass-produced clothing is widely available and supplants the old apparel, as cotton once replaced bark. The abrupt adoption of new styles signifies a society in rapid transition, with immensely broadened horizons, abandoning its sources.

THE LONGHOUSE ARTS AND CRAFTS, SIBU, SARAWAK

Dressed in her wedding garb, this wealthy young Iban woman displays an extensive amount of silver and gold jewelry, including an elaborate head-dress, earrings, bracelets, belts, a bag, anklets, and numerous coins sewn onto her skirt. A beaded neck piece and a Western-style watch complete the outfit.

Notes

1.

Despite the modern political division of Borneo between Indonesia and Malaysia, homogeneous tribes live on both sides of the border. The Ot Danum inhabit a large tract of southern Kalimantan (Indonesian Borneo), while the Bahau and Apo Kayan are found, respectively, along the Mahakam (Kutei) and Kayan rivers in northeastern Kalimantan. The Iban live primarily in the Kapuas River district of western Kalimantan from whence, during the past two centuries, they have migrated to the Lupar, Saribas, and (by the late nineteenth century) Rejang river systems of Sarawak (East Malaysia).

2.

Heine-Geldern, pp. 12-16.

3.

Ikat fragments allegedly manufactured in China (where the technique is no longer practiced) and preserved in the eighth-century imperial treasury Shoso-in at Nara (Japan) depict anthropomorphs markedly similar to more recent figural ikats of Sumba, Timor, Celebes, Mindanao, Borneo, and other insular weaving regions. See Schuster, pp. 339-68.

4.

Heine-Geldern, p. 15.

5.

Since the majority of this material is Iban, the reader is referred to the fine technical information regarding materials and process in Haddon and Start, pp. 5-22.

6.

Ibid., p. 4.

7.

A number of widespread regional practices appear to have lapsed among the Iban. Spenser St. John, writing in 1862, mentions that before a corpse was buried, dressed "in its finest garments, and often, if a man, fully armed... the body is rolled up in cloths and fine mats, kept together by pieces of bamboo tied on with rattan," which suggests conformity with the common Indonesian custom (cf. Sumba, Celebes) of wrapping the dead in shrouds, likely to have been *pua* (St. John, *Life in the Forests of the Far East,* vol. 1, Kuala Lumpur: Oxford University Press, 1974, p. 57).

8.

At the end of the nineteenth century a Sarawak government servant, Charles Hose, assembled a large and representative collection of Iban textiles and made meticulous inquiry regarding the names of individual designs. The Hose textiles, now mainly in The British Museum (Museum of Mankind), often bear as many as fifty labels identifying motifs as birds, insects, animals, plants, manmade implements, natural phenomena, and anthropomorphic spirits. Unfortunately, Hose did not or could not record the metaphorical meaning of these designs. In their catalog of a more recent Hose collection of early twentieth-century cloths in the Cambridge University Museum of Archaeology and Ethnology, Haddon and Start conscientiously report and categorize Hose's data. Their book is important as the only early published source of local information about these motifs.

9.

The early literature speaks of taking heads to acquire slaves in the next world and also as an act proving manhood or exacting revenge. It is likely, if comparison with other Indonesian cultures is valid, that originally headhunting was mainly one symbolic act among many that dramatized the tribal consciousness of death and rebirth.

10.

Haddon and Start.

43

14

Pua (ceremonial cloth)
Tributary of the Rejang River, Sarawak,
Malaysian Borneo (Iban)
Warp ikat, supplementary weft
Cotton
Warp: 223.7 cm.; weft: 127 cm.
Los Angeles County Museum of Art
Costume Council Fund
M.73.73.26

Soft-edged, large, relaxed patterns
dyed in atypical earthy brown and
black colors enhance the uncommon beauty of this cloth. Lines are
broad, filling but not crowding the
space. The mirror-image composition, unusual in Iban textiles, gives
harmony to the piece. Many of the
designs readily suggest (to both
modern Iban and outsiders)
abstract human faces and figures,
whose eyes, limbs, and ornaments
are fashioned from spirals and
S-shapes.

Pua (ceremonial cloth)
Niah River, Sarawak, Malaysian Borneo
(Iban)
Warp ikat, supplementary weft
Cotton
Warp: 212.7 cm.; weft: 91.4 cm.
Los Angeles County Museum of Art
Costume Council Fund
M.77.106.2

This small *pua,* though of much
more recent manufacture, exhibits
continuity with the traditions of
the oldest types, for example no. 21.
The pattern, with spreading tree
forms filling the center, describes a
tree "entirely illuminated by innumerable fireflies which emit their
light in rhythmic pulsations of in-
tensity."[1] Birds, shrews, and lizards
inhabit the foliage. The jagged
white shapes of the bottom border
are unusual, and T. T. Saklofsky has
suggested that these might represent stalagmites, which are found
in caves along the Niah River.

1.
Haddon and Start, p. 117.

16
Bidang (woman's skirt cloth), detail
Sarawak, Malaysian Borneo (Iban)
Warp ikat
Cotton
Warp: 108 cm.; weft: 57.2 cm.
Los Angeles County Museum of Art
Costume Council Fund
M.73.73.27

Abstracted zoomorphs such as these are a common design on *bidang*. Here the ikat is detailed and precise, largely due to the use of fine, commercially spun yarn. Because this yarn is thin, it is generally used double, which gives the design more definition. Wide stripe borders of brightly colored commercial threads began to appear on *bidang* as early as 1880, when commercially dyed threads became available in some areas of Borneo.

MHK

17

Bidang (woman's skirt cloth)
Mahakam, Indonesian Borneo (Bahau)
Warp ikat
Bast fiber, cotton
Warp: 103 cm.; weft: 73 cm.
Los Angeles County Museum of Art
Costume Council Fund
M.77.81.26

Speckled birds (?) in streamlined bands swoop across this typical Bahau bast fiber ikat. The sometimes odd color schemes (here emphasizing green and pink); a sharp angularity of design; and crisp, energetic imagery readily identify these relatively scarce weavings. The dotting throughout the reserved portions is an archaic feature, also remembered in a few islands of far eastern Indonesia.

18
Pua (ceremonial cloth)
Upper Rejang River, Sarawak,
Malaysian Borneo (Iban)
Warp ikat
Cotton
Warp: 251.5 cm.; weft: 152.4 cm.
Don R. Bierlich, Pacific Basin Services

Although the overall effect of this
vivid, large-scale *pua* suggests
flame or a snakeskin, Charles Hose
records similar patterns as representations of "tiger cats," their
diamond-shaped bodies enclosed by
the spotted pelt of the clouded
tiger (*Felis nebulosa*).

19
Pua (ceremonial cloth)
Rumah Nanka Gaat, Gaat River,
Sarawak, Malaysian Borneo
Warp ikat
Cotton
Warp: 244.5 cm.; weft: 137.2 cm.
Los Angeles County Museum of Art
Costume Council Fund
M.76.124
(See color plate, p. 15)

This large *pua* reflects both the
weaver's understanding of design
and a link with her artistic heritage: the interlocked figures that
flow throughout the design are
combined with key and rhomb
motifs preserved from the ancient
Dongson culture. This *pua* invoked
spiritual assistance in regenerating
the dwindling population; stylized
women are portrayed in the act of
giving birth, their wombs blessed
with two and sometimes
four infants.

T. T. Saklofsky

20
Dilak Bedong (sash), detail
Sarawak, Malaysian Borneo (Iban)
Supplementary weft on plain weave
Cotton, silk, gilt threads
Warp: 248.9 cm.; weft: 31.8 cm.
Los Angeles County Museum of Art
Gift of Mary Jane Leland
EX.77.260

Three rows of stylized figures interspersed with rows of abstract
geometric motifs adorn both ends
of this long, bright red sash. In the
bottom row two figures alternate
with small plantlike forms; the
center row portrays a more
abstracted series of anthropomorphs
with either horns or a headdress;
the inverted figures in the top row
are the most detailed, their costumes including an elaborate head-
dress and long earrings. Supplementary weft is also used on
women's skirts (*bidang*) and often,
as here, results in imagery and texture markedly different from that
of Iban ikat, with designs standing
out sharply in an orderly field and
bands separating one motif
from another.

21

Pua (ceremonial cloth)
Sarawak, Malaysian Borneo (Iban)
Warp ikat
Cotton
Warp: 327.7 cm.; weft: 152.4 cm.
Los Angeles County Museum of Art
Costume Council and Museum
Associates Purchase
M.77.113.1

This splendid *pua*, woven in the early twentieth century, displays an elegant asymmetrical flow from end to end. Motifs identified as tree trunks and branches laden with fruit and blossoms thread up and down to organize the composition. Reptiles wriggle in the side bands, while white lines separate the central tangle of forest from narrow bands at top and bottom that reportedly represent sheaves of young rice in areas cleared for its cultivation. Zippered bands of supplementary weft strengthen the warp ends. The ground color is deep burgundy, the result of many dyeings, and the ikat of fine hand-spun threads is precise.

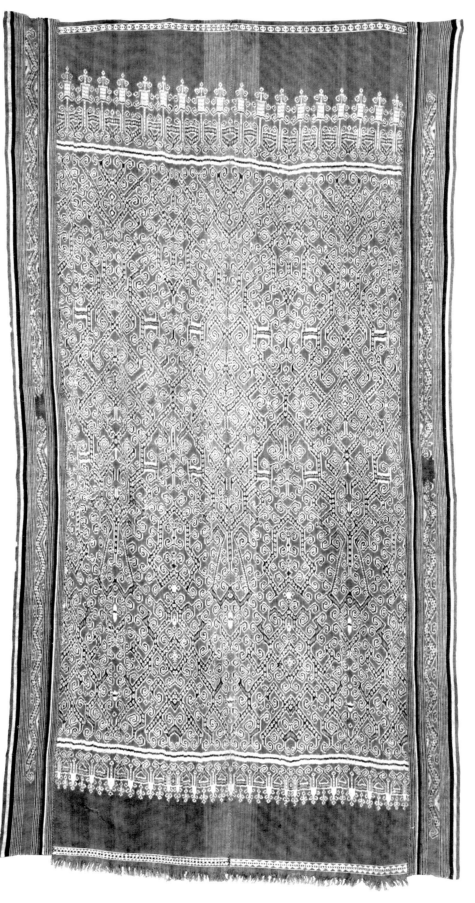

22

Pua (ceremonial cloth)
Sarawak, Malaysian Borneo (Iban)
Warp ikat, supplementary weft
Cotton
Warp: 202.6 cm.; weft: 116.2 cm.
Los Angeles County Museum of Art
Costume Council Fund
M.77.106.1

Machine-spun yarns account for the detail and precision in this ikat *pua*. The double lateral borders feature spotted crocodiles with tightly curled tails. The two end borders represent plants: the bottom probably showing a stylized root system, the top a stylized rice field. The design in the center field is referred to by Hose as an abstracted bird.

Anita Spertus and Jeff Holmgren

Celebes (*Sulawesi* in Indonesian), situated immediately east of Borneo, occupies a central position in the Malay Archipelago. The gregarious seagoing peoples who inhabit the island's four peninsulas have long maintained farflung trade and political contacts. Communities of Muslim Bugis and Makassarese from southwestern Celebes are found on every important Indonesian island, in Malaya, and even in Chinese cities; between the arrival of Islam in Celebes ca. 1600 and the end of Bugis political power in Malaya and Borneo two centuries later, they controlled the seas and established coastal outposts from east Java to the Moluccas and Timor. An international Hindu-Muslim flavor infused their crafts: rich brocades and gold embroideries, silver filigreed metalware, refined silks. From the late seventeenth century large populations and important natural resources attracted Dutch attention, to the northern (Minahasa) and southwestern peninsulas in particular; these two regions are presently among the most cosmopolitan in Indonesia.

Surrounded by these outgoing, artistically syncretic people, and in sharp contrast to them, the Toraja ("highlanders") inhabit the mountainous central portion of Celebes, where the four peninsulas meet. Isolated and sheltered by their extremely rugged environment, the Toraja maintained virtually unaltered a Bronze Age society and animist religious practice well into the twentieth century. Their distinctive textiles, rooted in an early phase of Indonesian culture, represent Celebes in this survey.

Dutch missionaries first penetrated Toraja in the 1890s. Colonial administration, established in the following twenty years, was superficial: few roads were built, and huge tracts of primeval forest and swamp were simply charted "unknown" or "uninhabited" before the advent of aerial survey. Not until the civil wars of the 1950s and early '60s, when conservative anti-Sukarno rebels sought refuge in Toraja, were Islam or Christianity imposed upon the tribes; today only the Sa'dan Toraja of Rantepao District still resist pressure to adopt an "established" faith.

The old religion (very much within living memory) reflects some Hindu ideas and terminology, but this connection seems remote, more tangential than parental. A few material remnants of ancient (ca. eighth century) Hindu high culture have been recovered in adjacent coastal districts of central Celebes. It is likely that while the island was Islamicized during the sixteenth and seventeenth centuries, Hindu-Buddhist refugees settled among the Toraja; Muslim Mandar and Bugis peoples bordering Toraja still refer to upland animist believers as "orang Buda." A more intimate and influential relation with the neighboring cultures of Borneo appears in similarity of racial type as well as in some striking coincidences of ornamental—especially textile—design: virtually all important Toraja patterns also occur among the Iban or Apo Kayan.

The overriding feature of Toraja religion was belief in the continuous and controlling presence in spirit of ancestors. Existing in both the upper and lower worlds, these spirits assisted (or thwarted) the living in all activities, and their intentions were thus of basic concern to the tribe. Proper respect for the dead was particularly important during the often lengthy period between death and final funeral rites, when danger to the community arising from malignant spirits was considered most acute. Magnificent ikats woven by two remote Toraja tribes served as funerary bindings (although also used as everyday apparel among non-weaving Toraja tribes to whom they were sold). When the deceased was well-born or highly honored, several ikats were wrapped tightly about the body; ordinary people received only one cloth, which they usually had acquired or made at an early age and reserved throughout life for this ultimate function.

The bold and graphic textiles for which the Toraja are noted were produced in the small southern valleys of Rongkong and Karataun (Mangki), the latter known generally by the name of a nearby Dutch administrative center, Galumpang.[1] It is indicative of the isolation of Toraja's many valleys that these striking weavings were not identified by scholars until around 1920. Although individual examples of this cloth had entered European museums and private collections, they had been erroneously attributed to the Bugis or to entirely different islands (Borneo, Bali). Authorities such as the missionaries A. C. Kruyt and N. Adriani, who had lived in central Celebes for a quarter-century and had established the fundamental ethnography of the region in voluminous publications, wrote as late as 1921 that "weaving in Toraja is nowhere indigenous."[2] Yet, since the mid-nineteenth century Dutch textile merchants had been producing, in Holland, machine-printed imitations of Toraja beeswax batik on cotton from authentic specimens in their possession, specifically for the Toraja trade.[3]

Three main categories of Toraja textiles are of particular interest: ikat of the warp, beeswax batik, and painted brushwork, all on cotton. In addition, clothing made with applied patches of brightly colored foreign cloth or bead and shell work is observed, as well as *plangi* banners, tablet-woven sashes, supplementary weft loincloths and betel pouches, and an extremely rare headcloth produced by the tapestry technique.

Most impressive are the funeral ikats, giant in scale and powerful in their visual clarity. Distinct from the netlike ebb and flow of Borneo textiles, and totally removed from refined floral or *patola*-based patterns that attest Indian influence, these cloths express neolithic angularity and strength—the signature of Toraja design—and evidence a culture still in touch with primal concepts. In one fundamental genre of ikat an energy field of small arrowlike elements pulses on the surface (see no. 26). Another, monumental type displays a "body" with four limbs (the *sekong*) flexing in the surrounding space (see nos. 24,27). In a third class, of great length (fifteen feet or more), serial designs in horizontal bands press against dramatic striped borders. The best of these ikats present positive and negative, foreground and background, with equal visual weight. The center field is often asymmetrically disposed within borders, which thus appear to crop an endlessly recurring design. Early specimens may add, along either side of the central panel, subtly striped bands (*kaki*, "feet") modulating in width and hue with gentle rhythm; the impression is of luxurious proportion and (in the overall context of Indonesian textiles) astonishing size.

Like other Indonesian peoples utilizing ancient ornamentation, the Toraja can no longer identify with convincing consistency the meanings that patterns may once have possessed. Carl Schuster and J. H. Jager Gerlings have proposed that a key design element, which occurs on many ikats, represents interlocked tiers of human bodies, arranged one above the other, sometimes headless except for the topmost figure.[4] Their analysis depends upon eliminating extraneous ornamentation in order to reveal the basic anthropomorphic figure.[5] In no. 24, for example, one stick figure stands over another with an enlarged diamond-shaped belly, while a third inverted figure shares the limbs of the upright one. This interpretation gains support from a comparison with Iban and Apo Kayan textiles, which present the same figural motifs more clearly.[6] Understood thus, the Toraja funeral ikats display a field of ancestor figures, metaphorically protecting and guiding the spirit they enwrap.

Evidently arising from a different tradition than these schematic anthropomorphs, literally described humans and crocodiles do appear, though very rarely, on early Toraja ikats from Rongkong.[7] They are encountered often, however, in darkened silhouette, on the mysterious and magical beeswax batik banners and shamans' cloths. These cloths, believed to be of heavenly origin, are greatly treasured. The banners typically fly from tall poles on ceremonial occasions, although old photographs record their use as sashes and as head cloths (the latter reportedly reserved for successful headhunters). The often close relationship of the batik designs to carvings adorning ceremonial houses in the Sa'dan (Rantepao) District suggests a provenance within that region. Production ceased early in the twentieth century.

Several principal types of beeswax batik banners may be distinguished: earliest and most compelling, a deep-dyed "black" variety of a freely drawn, pictorial nature; an indigo-colored version, refined but far more controlled and measured; and the block-printed indigo and white imitations, mechanical in appearance, reportedly manufactured in Holland.

Shamans' cloths (see no. 25) were executed both in batik and in painted brushwork. The oldest examples (black and ocher on handspun natural cotton) occasionally bear designs identical with those on decorated barkcloth, which was produced, until the beginning of the twentieth century, in northern and eastern Toraja. Buffalo are central to the design of typical shamans' cloths. A coral and turquoise variety occurs in southern Toraja; usually on milled cotton, the unusual colors and rather stiff patterning suggest more recent manufacture.

Quality textile production effectively ceased in Toraja with the Japanese occupation and the civil upheavals following independence. Antique specimens remaining in Toraja are now extremely scarce[8] because both Rongkong and Karataun were destroyed as tactical anti-guerrilla policy during the 1950s and their inhabitants either evacuated to the coast or gathered in protective enclaves. Since returning to their valleys, Toraja weavers have renewed ikat work on a small scale, geared to export trade with Rantepao rather than local ritual use. Contemporary examples, using harsh and fugitive chemical dyes, are coarse in pattern and texture.

Notes

1.
One other important center of cotton
ikat, not Torajanese, was located near
Bentenan, northern Celebes. Perhaps
two dozen examples survive in museum
collections. Typical are women's sarongs
depicting wide-eyed crouching frontal
humans, like those of Mindanao,
Borneo, and Timor. Production ceased
ca. 1880.
2.
Van Nouhuys, 1921, p. 237.
3.
Van Nouhuys, 1925, pp. 118-19.
4.
Schuster and Jager Gerlings, especially
pp. 106-28.
5.
Schuster, ibid., discusses clear prototyp-
ical designs from other, generally ancient cultures in widely separated parts
of Asia (Siberia, Afghanistan, the
Caucasus, China, etc.) that correspond
closely to Toraja patterns, revealing a
common anthropomorphic basis.
6.
Jager Gerlings, pls. 27, 30, and figs. 21,
22, 26.
7.
See the exhibition catalog *Indonesië-
Oceanië*, Rotterdam Museum voor
Land- en Volkenkunde, 1965, pls. 12
and 13, as well as a textile in the
Rijksmuseum voor Volkenkunde,
Leiden, and others in several Dutch
private collections.
8.
Extraordinary collections of early Toraja
textiles are preserved in the Tropen-
museum, Amsterdam; the Museum für
Völkerkunde, Basel; and the Museum
voor Land- en Volkenkunde, Rotterdam.

Sarita (pennant)
Rantepao, central Celebes (Toraja)
Batik
Cotton
Warp: 655.3 cm.; weft: 25.4 cm.
Los Angeles County Museum of Art
Costume Council Fund
M.77.91.1

Now hung as flying banners at
ceremonial events, long narrow
"magic" cloths of this type previously served as sashes and head
cloths. Among the various bands of
traditional patterns that divide the
length into small units is a pictorial section, in this case representing a water buffalo with great
horns being paraded prior to sacrifice. Among the Toraja people
ownership of such a beast is an indication of both wealth and high
ritual status. The freely drawn designs on these cloths seem to
resemble carvings on ceremonial
houses in the Toraja Rantepao District.   MHK

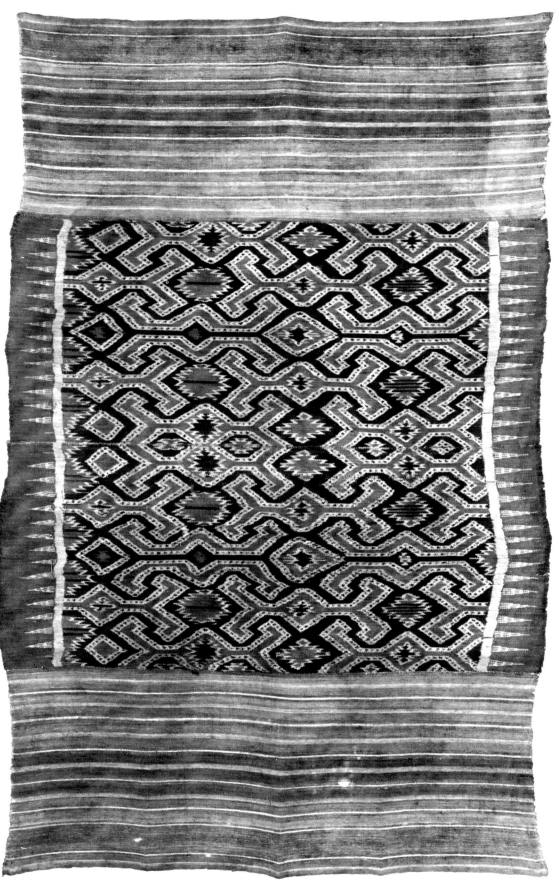

Lelesepun (funeral shroud)
Galumpang, central Celebes (Toraja)
Warp ikat
Cotton
Warp: 148.5 cm.; weft: 237.7 cm.
Costume Council and Museum
Associates Purchase
TR.2191.1

Bold geometric designs, possibly representing ancestor figures, fill the center field of this textile. The basic *sekong* element, a diamond-shaped "body" with four limbs flexing inward, has been used from ancient times throughout and beyond Asia, though seldom on such a monumental scale. Cropped by striped borders at the margins, the *sekong* can be read from any direction and in both the dark and light shades, interlocking like the unending genealogy they purportedly symbolize.

25

Mawa' (shaman's cloth)
Makale, Rantepao, central Celebes
(Toraja)
Stamped and painted cotton
Warp: 330.2 cm.; weft: 74.3 cm.
Steven G. Alpert
EX.77.233

Although this composition revolves around a small double-gated enclosure encircled by marching ducks and a herder, it is the flowing, forested fields at either side that compel immediate attention. Gentle, wavy groves of trees intermingle with two-tone printed crosses, symbols of plenty. Believed to be "heaven sent," these shamans' cloths convey a direct visual language unlike any other Indonesian textile.

26

Porisitutu' (funeral shroud)
Rongkong, central Celebes (Toraja)
Warp ikat
Cotton
Warp: 170.1 cm.; weft: 264.1 cm.
Los Angeles County Museum of Art
Costume Council Fund
M.77.20.2
(See color plate, p. 16)

This fine shroud, probably dating to the second quarter of the present century, displays several unusual features. Tree shapes in the center section rise in peaked triangles, suggesting a link with the mountain forms encountered on textiles from the Lesser Sunda Islands, notably Lomblen. The square middle panel is bordered by delicate round blossoms, dotted like the back and wings of a Celebes beetle and interspersed with stars. Soft shades of indigo enrich the surface, while on the outside edges broad swaths of color add dimension to the textile.

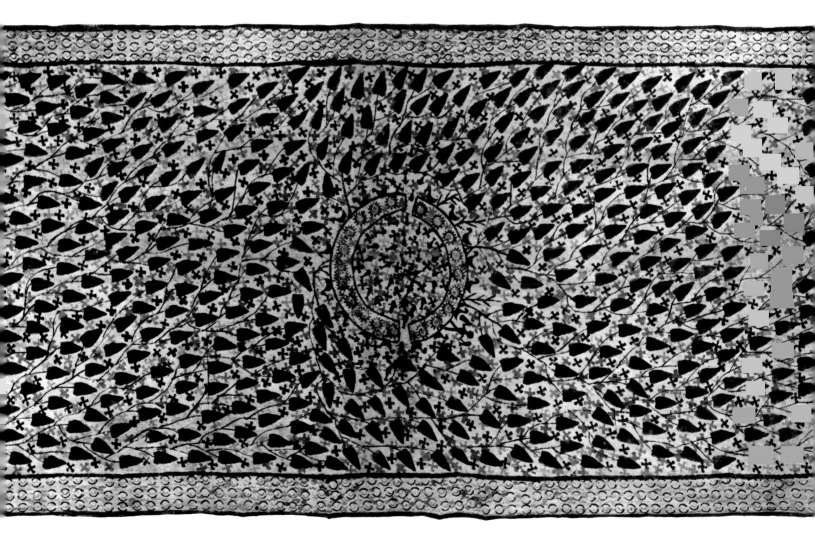

27

Sekomandi (fragment of a funeral shroud)
Galumpang, central Celebes (Toraja)
Warp ikat
Cotton
Warp: 106.7 cm.; weft: 61 cm.
Anita Spertus and Jeff Holmgren
EX.77.312

This remarkable fragment exemplifies the aesthetic richness of the earliest surviving Toraja textiles. One-fourth its original size, it possibly dates to the third quarter of the nineteenth century. The four limbs of the *sekong* are lanky and curl inward several times under tension; in more recent examples (cf. no. 24) the limbs are truncated and rigid. The unusual use of blue on the interior of the arms modulates the background and suggests depth. Blunt black teeth surround the perimeter of the *sekong*; in opposition, red teeth contain and dramatize the design. In a few places the cooling white outlines are omitted and a red splash sits like a hot coal on the black surface. Crosses, symbols of abundance, appear in the margins. Lines are still supple, relaxed, in the spirit of the early Borneo textiles to which the cloth relates; the solidification into hard linearity came later, during the first part of the twentieth century.

Bronwen and Garrett Solyom

Javanese batik is the richest and most complex of all wax-resist textiles. This complexity derives not only from the myriad patterns, colors, and styles, but also from the social, religious, economic, and aesthetic values associated with it. Reflecting Java's own crowded history, the batik's symbols and their underlying philosophy must be interpreted on many levels, like the batik patterning itself, with one form overlaying another or one shape fitting within the next. Whether from village or court, a batik may proclaim its unmistakable Javanese identity but still bear motifs and elements of style of distinct Chinese, Indian, European, or Islamic lineage. Javanese batik displays a range of developmental stages from peasant simplicity to classic refinement; it shows extensive regional variation and permits a wealth of personal interpretation from the makers; and yet all batik from this area still retains certain distinctive elements in common. It forms an integral part of a culture shared by millions of people.

Javanese batik is usually made by applying liquid wax as a pattern-shaping resist on fine cotton cloth, or sometimes on silk. (One important exception is an isolated batik tradition in far west Java, where rice flour paste is used instead of wax.) The cloth is generally machine loomed, of varying grades, formerly mostly imported. Sometimes a coarser handspun and hand-woven material is encountered. The wax (beeswax, paraffin, resin, etc.) may be applied with a wax pen *(canting)* or with a copper stamp *(cap).* A distinction may thus be made between *tulis* batik, hand written with the *canting,* and *cap* batik, made with the stamp. Sometimes both methods may be combined on the same cloth. In the conservative Javanese view, the refinement of the best *tulis* is most highly valued. Observation, however, shows some village women wearing *tulis* of a more cursory and direct kind, briskly sketched with a *canting* of larger size and often dyed only blue on white. This suggests a lively folk batik tradition that appears to have received little attention.

Depending on the number of colors, the cloth may be waxed, then immersed in dye several times, the wax being either partially or completely removed after each step by scraping or boiling. There are numerous local variants of the process, including painting the dye on rather than immersing the cloth in it, especially for small areas of color. Top dyeing, the application of a second dye over an area already dyed another color, is sometimes done. Since early in this century, easy and efficient imported chemical dyes have increased the palette available to the designer and now almost totally replace the often more subtle vegetable colors. Occasionally brown is still obtained from *soga,* a traditional dye made from a mixture of wood and bark.

Like performing traditional music, dance, or drama, or forging the traditional weapon, the *keris,* making *tulis* batik was a spiritual discipline.[1] Mastery of both mind and body was requisite for the work, when a single *kain* might take months of painstaking effort to complete. There would

be long hours of sitting on the floor, tending a charcoal brazier, meticulously waxing the repeating, often minute, motifs. First one side of the cloth was waxed, then the other, matching line for line and dot for dot to assure maximum clarity of the pattern after dyeing. Achieving the appropriate state of body and mind was sometimes aided by the surrounding "spiritual climate." A Surakarta batik designer, R. T. Hardjonagoro, recalls the sight of hundreds of women working for his grandfather, dressed neatly in jackets and batik or hand-loomed skirt cloths, with jewelry such as the large traditional earplugs. They would sit cross-legged or with their legs folded under them, chanting time-honored melodies while they worked. The scrape and wash workers would hum narrative and mood songs from the shadow plays, to the tapping of their resonant rhythms.[2] Even today fine batik embodies something of the atmosphere of such workshops.

While mostly for everyday wear, batik is part of ceremonial or formal costume as well. Today it is also often designed to be made into Western-style shirts and dresses. While these fashions change, the basic rectangular and square forms of traditional garments remain constant. Their proportions and the ways in which they are worn clearly affect the arrangement of the patterns on them.

The *kain panjang* (see nos. 28, 32-34, 37), or more simply, *kain* (approximately 2½-3 x 1 m.) is an ankle-length skirt cloth, usually worn by women. It is wrapped with the left end overlapping the right, sometimes with narrow knife pleats arranged in front. For formal occasions in central Java, men may also wear the *kain,* wrapped more loosely, right end over left, with broader pleats in front. They may add a batik *belangkon,* an intricately folded turbanlike hat that is sewn from an *iket,* or man's headcloth (about 1 x 1 m.). The *iket* is still occasionally tied by hand rather than sewn.

Especially along the north coast both men and women wear the sarong, a versatile skirt cloth (about 2 x 1 m.) frequently sewn into a tube. The distinguishing feature of Javanese sarongs is the *kepala,* literally the "head," a rectangular section spanning the sarong from selvage to selvage. The color and pattern differ from the "body" of the cloth, giving it a special focus. The *kepala* may be worn at the back, or at the side, or inside the front folds. Combined with a lace or embroidered overblouse, the sarong was a favored garment of Dutch and Eurasian women in colonial times; it is also popular with Chinese Javanese women. In central Java today it is principally worn by men, who also may wrap it round their shoulders as a mantle or draw it over their heads against the cold. It also frequently serves as a sleeping garment.

Another flexible and ubiquitous garment is the *slendang* (see nos. 31, 39), or shoulder cloth (about 2-3½ m. x 60 cm.). The shorter ones, folded over the right shoulder to the left hip, complement the overblouse, or *kebaya*, as part of women's formal dress. The longer ones are indispensable as slings for carrying babies or baskets. Knotted at one end to hold money and other small items, they may serve as a purse as well.

The *kemben*, or breast cloth, is related in form to the *slendang* and may have developed from it.[3] Worn instead of a blouse, or under a blouse, it is rarely seen today except on older women in the villages, on dancers, or within the central Javanese courts, where it is still part of the daily attire of female court attendants.

Indeed, the costumes of the courts and the dance show some of the older, more complex elements of Javanese dress. The *dodot* (see no. 35), a huge cloth almost four times the size of a *kain*, was once worn principally by officials and members of the court, draped and folded as an overskirt. In the etiquette of the courts, each person is defined by his dress. *Dodot* worn by members of the royal family must therefore be of surpassing quality and display the finest batik artistry.[4]

The degree to which the Javanese value batik may be seen in several ways. For many, fine batik is a luxury article. A good piece, made by a relative and kept within a family for special occasions, becomes a source of prestige, a precious family heirloom. It is safeguarded and seldom worn; in times of need it can be sold or pawned.[5] Batik may also function in a symbolic context related to the ritual importance of yarn, the process of weaving, and woven cloth itself in Javanese culture. Thomas Stamford Raffles, for example, describes how in the early nineteenth century a hank of cotton yarn was part of the ritual marriage fee paid to the officiating priest.[6] For the *selamatan tingkeban*, a ceremony held in the seventh month of pregnancy to prepare for the birth of a first child, some yarn and a shuttle may form part of the ritual offering. Similarly, a piece of batik placed in a bamboo tube may be included in a special offering for the "meeting ceremony" of a wedding.[7]

The origins of the batik technique in Java are obscure. The word itself is both Javanese and Malay-Indonesian and was first recorded in early seventeenth-century Dutch texts describing a shipload of fabrics with colored patterns,[8] but the earliest extant pieces probably date from after 1750.[9] Certainly foreign influences have long been felt in the patterns, if not in the technique. Since a lively textile trade flourished for centuries between India, China, and Southeast Asia, a mutual exchange of influences probably occurred. The floral and geometric patterns of the blocked resist prints from India's Coromandel coast left their mark, though perhaps less pervasively than *patola*, the double-ikat silk from Gujarat. *Patola* was also called *cinde* in Java, where it was imported in some quantity and highly treasured.[10] In the courts it was used for costumes and a variety of other items. There are batik patterns named for their allusion to *patola: cinde wilis, cinde kenanga,* and *cinde parang.*[11] Some

batiks share with *patola* and certain other Indian textiles the floral-geometric center-field patterns and the division of the cloth by side and end borders, the latter often incorporating the common *tumpal* motif.

Before the spread of chemical dyes, each region had its characteristic colors, achieved through well-guarded formulas and processes passed on through families for generations. Unusual or even "magical" ingredients such as brown palm sugar, fermented cassava, varieties of banana, or even shredded chicken might be included in the dye recipes to enhance, for instance, the deep luster of indigo.[12] Each region had its distinctive patterns as well. With chemical dyes, however, exclusive regional possession of color and pattern combinations was technologically at an end, and identifying the provenance of an individual piece of batik has thus become more difficult. Nevertheless, two major style areas can be distinguished: first, the central Javanese regions around the court centers of Surakarta (Solo) and Jogjakarta and, second, the various town centers spread along almost the entire north coast of the island, including a small inland area around Tasikmalaya.

The classic batiks of central Java are distinguished by rich brown and blue tones—originally *soga* and indigo—combined with white for Jogjakarta or cream for Surakarta. The patterns and their manner of execution speak of a long evolution. Typically, patterns, particularly the geometric ones, are dense, refined, and controlled, showing an extraordinarily sensitive dialogue between figure and ground, positive and negative. The backgrounds are either undyed (cream or white), blue black from brown dyed over blue, or brown.

The batiks of the north coast employ a broader vocabulary of color and form and share an organic liveliness of composition. Major patterns are often larger, with more fluid, curvilinear elaboration. There is less emphasis on a strongly controlled pattern field—the motifs may be placed on a plain ground or against a smaller ground pattern, relating easily to each other in a more spontaneous way. Because north coast-style batiks constitute a large, heterogeneous group, they may be further subdivided geographically—for example, into those from Cirebon, a court center, and those from other main centers such as Pekalongan. They seem to reflect the polyglot makeup of the coastal population and the greatly varying cultural forces exerted on the region through history: Chinese, Islamic, central Javanese, and European.

There are thousands of batik patterns, with new ones being invented all the time. Popular motifs appear with innumerable variations and classifying them is an endless challenge.[13] A general division is made between geometric and non-geometric. The many families of geometric patterns include variations of the swastika, *banji;* those inspired by weaving and plaitwork, *nitik;* those based on diagonal stripes, *garis miring;* those based on squares and triangles, for example, *tambal* and *slobok;* and those falling into grid systems of circles, lozenges, squares, etc., called *ceplok*. Non-geometric patterns include the very broad category *semen,* which refers to buds and sprouts, and thus to tendril and leaf motifs as well. There are many profuse floral patterns. A most interesting design complex characteristic of Cirebon is that which suggests elements of a garden scene—gates, pavilions, lotus pools, with birds, animals, trees, and mountains—perhaps a representation of a cosmic landscape. Chinese-style rock and cloud configurations are also popular. Other pictorial types include those with processions and tableaus of *wayang* figures.

Certain batik patterns have acquired special associations and importance. In some instances it is customary for the bride's family to give the groom a *kain* with *sidomukti,* a type of *ceplok* pattern. It is worn for the *upacara temu,* or "ritual meeting" portion of the marriage proceedings. Since this *kain* is one of a pair, it becomes known as *sawitan,* one of "matching elements."[14] When they ritually receive the couple, the parents of the bride also wear *sawitan,* frequently in the small, geometric *truntum* pattern.[15]

From at least the eighteenth century certain patterns became the appanage of royalty. By decree of the sultan of Jogjakarta, for example, the *parang rusak barong* pattern was restricted for his use and that of his chief consort and of the crown prince and his spouse. On holy days when the sultan wore the pattern, it had to be a faultlessly executed example; no bleeding of color through cracks in the wax was permitted as this would constitute a flaw, destroying the magic power with which the cloth was believed to be charged.

A batik with the same pattern was also part of a ritual offering made to the spirits of the sultan's ancestors.[16] Apparently, from the court point of view such restricted patterns were appropriate only for a sacred and divine king and thus had extraordinary power, meaning, and feeling. These restrictions are relaxed today and other Javanese may wear the patterns outside the palace walls, although they would probably not do so if they were to enter the courts themselves.

The textiles illustrated here show only a tantalizing cross-section of the rich spectrum of Javanese batiks.

His Royal Highness, Sri Sultan Hamengku Buwono VII of Jogjakarta (1877-1921), sits in state beside some of his court regalia. He wears a batik kain *with the restricted* parang rusak barong *pattern over* patola *silk trousers. His jacket of triangular patchwork,* tambalan, *is a sacred heirloom with its own title,* Kyai Antakusuma.

Notes

1.
Clifford Geertz, *The Religion of Java,* The Free Press of Glencoe, 1960, p. 287.

2.
R. T. Hardjonagoro, "Excerpt of a Talk Given by Raden Tumenggung Hardjonagoro of Solo for the Guests of SRIHANA, Jakarta, March 7, 1977," typescript, p. 2.

3.
Veldhuisen-Djajasoebrata, p. 26.

4.
Ibid.

5.
Geertz, *Religion,* p. 65.

6.
Thomas Stamford Raffles, *The History of Java,* vol. 1, 1817, reprint, Kuala Lumpur: Oxford University Press, 1965, p. 319.

7.
Geertz, *Religion,* pp. 42,58.

8.
Steinmann, 1947, p. 2091.

9.
Batiks, p. 8.

10.
Alfred Bühler, "Patola Influences in Southeast Asia," *Journal of Indian Textile History,* no. 4, 1959, p. 16.

11.
Ibid., p. 17, footnote 1.

12.
Tirta and Lau, p. 1.

13.
Compare, for example, the classifications suggested in Veldhuisen-Djajasoebrata; Steinmann, 1947; and Jasper and Pirngadie, 1916.

14.
Sidik Gondowarsito, "Sekelumit tentang tatajara adat dan upatjara pengantin Djawa," *Dian,* vol. 13, no. 3, 1965, p. 21.

15.
Ibid., p. 23.

16.
Veldhuisen-Djajasoebrata, p. 19.

28

Kain Panjang (skirt cloth)
North coast, Java
Batik
Cotton
Warp: 254 cm.; weft: 104.8 cm.
Los Angeles County Museum of Art
Costume Council Fund
M.77.71.1

Patterns with small linear motifs on a white ground are difficult to achieve in batik, but here the figures attain a filigree delicacy. The ground of this north coast *kain panjang* was waxed with a meticulous hand, and both the red and the subsidiary colors of black, blue, and green were dyed with great precision. A single fragile line encircles a stylized phoenix bird and peony blossoms. Ethereal deer orbit this central form, while two different potted plants complete the basic motif configuration, which clearly reflects a Chinese influence. In popular Chinese design such a constellation of symbols sometimes formed a rebus, with each symbol representing a word or phrase or together creating a phrase related to wishes for happiness, longevity, many children, etc. The individual figures also had a symbolic meaning: the phoenix stood for happiness, fertility, and good fortune; the deer for longevity, wealth, and dignity; the peony for love, affection, and feminine beauty. The roundel with the phoenix and peony is probably derived from Chinese porcelains but should not be confused with the very similar motif of a crane holding the peaches of immortality. The *tumpal* motif in the end border is a pan-Southeast Asian motif, well represented in Indonesian art; in its more complex forms it may be a blend of indigenous and imported elements. As a symbol, the *tumpal* seems to have been related to growth and fertility; the sacred mountain, Meru; and also perhaps to the tree of life, the lotus, and the lotus bud.

29

Sarong (skirt cloth)
North coast, Java
Batik, *prada*
Cotton
Warp: 203.2 cm.; weft: 109.2 cm.
Indianapolis Museum of Art
EX.77.294

In this sarong delicate birds and butterflies seem to blend softly into the encompassing leaves and tendrils. They share the linear fragility of a batik style seen particularly in such north coast cities as Tegal, Indramayu, and Jakarta and in some older central Javanese batiks as well. The phoenix birds reflect the Chinese influence that is preeminent on the coast. Phoenixes are known on sixteenth- and seventeenth-century "swatow group" Chinese porcelains and also on fifteenth- and sixteenth-century Annamese porcelains found in Indonesia.[1] In Java the phoenix, or *burung Hook,* retains some of its Chinese significance as an auspicious symbol (compare with a dif-

ferent representation of the phoenix in no. 28). The opposing rows of rectilinear *tumpal* on the blue ground of the *kepala* strongly contrast with the more organic patterns of the body. The motifs are all overlaid or highlighted with gold-leaf (or gold-dust) glue work called *prada.* Usually gilded on one side only, *prada* batiks occur both in central Java, where albumen is usually the adhesive, and on the north coast, where a mixture of linseed oil and resin may be used.

They were worn for high ceremonial occasions or festivals. The upper edge of this sarong, where it would be folded over or belted to keep it in place, has no gold. This reveals its basic blue on white color combination, called *biron* from *biru,* "blue"), one of four very general color types in Javanese batik. The other types are red on white (called *bangbangan* from *abang,* red), *soga* brown, and polychrome.

1.
E.W. van Orsoy de Flines, *Guide to the Ceramic Collection (Foreign Ceramics),* Jakarta: Museum Pusat, 1972, pp. 41, 44, 66-67.

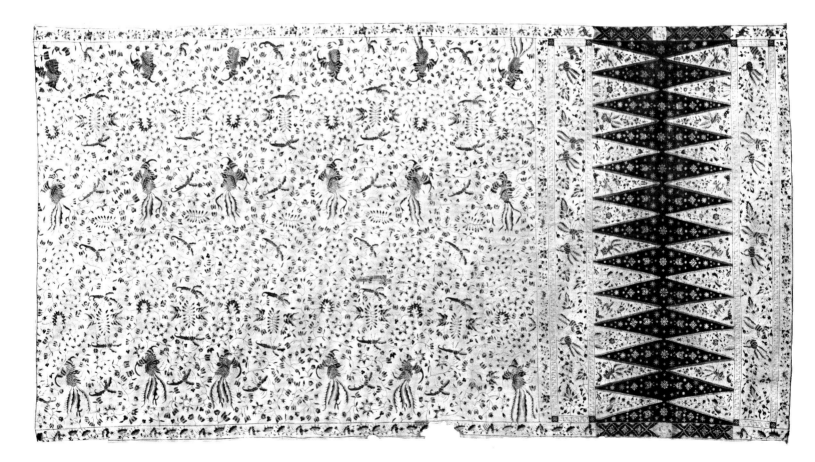

30

Sarong (skirt cloth)
North coast, Java
Batik
Cotton
Warp: 100.7 cm.; weft: 105.4 cm.
Los Angeles County Museum of Art
Wilma Leithead Wood Bequest
58.34.24

The best of the north coast style may be seen in the subtle colors and coherent design of this sarong. The body consists of a network of squares, each filled with a lively deer, bird, crab, turtle, or plant motif. The frame of the squares contains a geometric motif suggestive of a Chinese cloud pattern. The overall configuration of squares belongs to the *ceplokan* category, which comprises floral-geometric patterns based on circles, lozenges, squares, stars, etc., arranged with interstitial motifs to form a grid. The word derives from *ceplok,* which includes among its meanings the onomatopoeic one of flopping or plopping sounds. It is also the name for small polygonal metal plates with relief patterns that were used, for example, to close the end of a bolster cover.[1]

A deep *mengkudu* red over a tawny cream ground (the tawniness perhaps a by-product of the predyeing preparation of the cloth) is enlivened by the spare use of blue in this sarong. The *kepala* demonstrates a particularly successful balancing of the strong red center with the alternating blue and cream *tumpal.* As on many Javanese batiks, the selvages are patterned with fine stripes, apparently imitating a selvage treatment still found on many Indonesian woven textiles.

1.
R. J. Wilkinson, *A Malay–English Dictionary,* part 2, Mytilene: Salavopoulos and Kinderlis, 1932, p. 214.

31

Slendang (shoulder cloth)
North coast, Java
Batik
Silk
Warp: 315 cm.; weft: 52.1 cm.
Los Angeles County Museum of Art
Costume Council Fund
M.74.18.5

This *slendang,* probably from the
north coast, reflects the Javanese
fascination with complex layered
geometry. The pattern is drawn in
lines of "burnt brown," with accents of blue, on beige silk. It is an
extraordinarily involved *ceplokan*
type in which small repeating
forms are compounded into larger
forms. Every form is simultaneously a major element in at least
one design system and a minor
element in another, overlapping
system. In the dialogue between
them, neither the large nor small
forms dominate. They may
momentarily compete to catch the
eye as it shifts its focus, but the
overall organization is so deftly
manipulated that each element is
in dynamic balance and no single
system stands out. The ends have a
striped border in batik, imitating a
fringe, followed by an actual
twisted and knotted fringe. Silk
slendang are frequently referred to
as *lokcan* (sometimes translated as
lok, "blue," and *can,* "silk").
Usually made or ordered by the
Chinese Javanese, they were also
exported from Java and were particularly popular in Bali. Those
with geometric patterns were less
common than those with phoenix
and plant motifs.

32

Kain Panjang (skirt cloth)
Java
Batik
Cotton
Warp: 251.4 cm.; weft: 106.7 cm.
Los Angeles County Museum of Art
Costume Council Fund
M.77.71.2
(See color plate, p. 17)

This *kain panjang* combines elements of both central Javanese and
north coast styles. It is of the type
called *tiga negeri,* which literally
means "three countries." These
batiks apparently began their pro-
cessing in Pekalongan, where the
floral and animal motifs, and probably the borders, were waxed and
dyed with *mengkudu,* a red vegetable dye. Next the unfinished *kain*
was sent to the city of Semarang,
also on the north coast, where the
background patterns were likely
waxed and dyed blue. Finally, in
Jogjakarta, the *kain* was dyed *soga*
brown and finished.[1] In this example the cloth is divided in half into
a *pagi-sore,* or "morning-evening,"
arrangement, providing the wearer
with a choice of pattern and color.
On one half large bouquets are surrounded by birds, butterflies, and
deer. On the other, similar bouquets
are imposed over an additional
background pattern: a blue lattice
of the *ceplokan* type, with small
blossoms, leaf sprays, and geese (or
swans) within its squares.

1.
Damais, pp. 12-13.

33

Kain Panjang (skirt cloth)
Atelier of E. Van Zuylen
Pekalongan, north coast, Java
Batik
Cotton
Warp: 106.7 cm.; weft: 232.1 cm.
Los Angeles County Museum of Art
Costume Council and Museum
Associates Purchase
TR. 2173.2

Little Red Riding Hood in her
European fairy-tale clothes stands
before the "wolf," actually a lion
closer in style to a Chinese *singha.*
The red floral edge border is a
common Pekalongan element, and
the geometric filling motif, *isen,* of
small striped squares is also frequently seen on the north coast.
Such eclecticism is one aspect of
the European influence on Javanese
batik; other fairy-tale subjects, such
as Snow White, are also known.
From the early twentieth century to
the Second World War a number of
ateliers run by Dutch and other
Europeans produced batiks blending local and imported motifs and
experimenting with new color
combinations. They catered not
only to the taste of colonial clien-
tele but also to European markets.
In this same period batik had a reciprocal influence in Europe, especially reflected in Dutch art
nouveau. This piece bears both a
signature in batik and the ink
stamp of the E. Van Zuylen atelier,
once in Pekalongan.

34

Kain Panjang (skirt cloth)
Jogjakarta, central Java
Batik
Cotton
Warp: 276 cm.; weft: 105.1 cm.
Los Angeles County Museum of Art
Gift of Sylvia, Nanies, and Gordon
Bishop
M.77.97

The immaculate white ground with classic *soga* brown and dark blue identifies this remarkable *kain panjang* with Jogjakarta. The technical mastery combined with the dramatic scale of the motifs further identifies it with the court. Indeed, the motifs both individually and in this combination were once re-

stricted to court use. This piece is said to have been made in the 1930s for Sultan Hamengku Buwono VIII. The paired wings with a fan tail are called *sawat.* Usually identified as a symbol of the *garuda,* or mythical eagle, it possibly also combines some characteristics of the peacock, a bird sometimes attributed magical powers. Close examination shows two birds' heads, with long crests on either side of the tail, indicating that the motif consists not of a single bird but of a pair. The *sawat* is imposed over a ground pattern of giant *kawung*—in this example, a system of ovals forming lozenges between them. The lozenges are so large that they are filled with patterned roundels. The motif in the roundels is a phoenix, much abstracted—a notable example of Chinese influence.[1] Groups of four

ovals can be seen as forming either a circle or a four-petaled blossom. This configuration is the special characteristic of *kawung.* It has been suggested that the four-petaled blossom represents a simplified lotus.[2] *Kawung* has also been associated with the dry leaf of the *areng* (*aren,* "sugar palm") and with the oval fruit of the kapok tree.[3] The two black crosses inside each oval suggest seeds not yet removed. A related meaning given for *kawung* is "cotton,"[4] which is regarded by the Javanese as so essential that, along with a sheaf of rice, it forms part of the symbol for clothing and food seen on the coats of arms of the Jogjakarta and Surakarta courts. Some variations of

kawung, especially the older ones, retain more of their circular character. It is an ancient motif, appearing, for example, on thirteenth-century east Javanese temple sculpture,[5] where it may represent textiles with gold-leaf glue work rather than batik.[6]

1.
Adam, p. 64 and fig. 43.
2.
Langewis and Wagner, p. 30.
3.
Bolland, Jager Gerlings, and Langewis, introduction, p. 4.
4.
L. Mardiwarsito, *Djawa Kuno Kawi-Indonesia,* Jakarta: n.p., 1969, p. K8.
5.
Langewis and Wagner, p. 30. Also Thomassen à Thuessink van der Hoop, pp. 80-81.
6.
Langewis and Wagner, p. 30.

35

Dodot (royal ceremonial garment)
Central Java
Batik, *prada*
Cotton
Warp: 350.5 cm.; weft: 213.4 cm.
Los Angeles County Museum of Art
Costume Council and Museum
Associates Purchase
TR.2186.1

This large cloth may be worn only
by the king, bride, groom, or dancers in the court of Surakarta. The
white rhomboid shape, *bangun,* and
the blue indigo symbolize water
and earth. The edge of the center
section is decorated with zigzag
tritik lines.   MHK

Kain Panjang (skirt cloth)
Jogjakarta, central Java
Batik
Cotton
Warp: 257.8 cm.; weft: 106.7 cm.
Gordon Bishop, Bishop International
EX.77.285

Like no. 34, this *kain* was said to be made in the 1930s for Sultan Hamengku Buwono VIII of Jogjakarta, and again the grand scale of the motifs confirms its probable court use. Rows of neatly dovetailing butterflies are separated by narrower but more powerful rows of *parang rusak (barong?)*. Much debate has occurred over the meaning of this name. The word *parang* appears in the fourteenth-century Javanese literary work *Nagara-Kertagama* in the form *parangmuka,* meaning "enemy."[1] The combination of *parang* with *rusak,* meaning "damaged" or "destroyed," may thus have carried the idea of "enemy destroying." Another interpretation arises from a literal translation of the words *parang,* meaning a "machetelike hacking knife," and *rusak*—thus the combination "broken knife." The name may also involve a distortion of the words *pelang rusak,*[2] meaning "broken ikat," or a pattern where the lines of color are interrupted.[3] The motif itself has even been linked with the lotus leaf[4] and with a New Guinea motif of birds' heads with long beaks.[5] Certainly in Southeast Asia the *parang*-type pattern is both old and well represented.[6]

1.
Theodore G. Pigeaud, *Java in the Fourteenth Century: A Study in Cultural History,* The Hague: Martinus Nijhoff, 1963, vol. 5, p. 348.
2.
Th. J. Veltman, "De Atjehsche Zijdeïndustrie," *Internationales Archiv für Ethnographie,* vol. 20, nos. 15-58, 1912, pp. 52-53.
3.
R. J. Wilkinson, *A Malay-English Dictionary,* part 2, Mytilene: Salavopoulos and Kinderlis, 1932, p. 231.
4.
Wagner, p. 25.
5.
Ibid., p. 26.
6.
Veldhuisen-Djajasoebrata, p. 19.

Kain Panjang (skirt cloth)
Jogjakarta, central Java
Batik
Cotton
Warp: 245.8 cm.; weft: 105.4 cm.
Kent Watters
EX.77.213

This *pagi-sore* batik, probably from Jogjakarta, presents an unusual synthesis of pictorial and geometric forms. Half the cloth is filled with alternating diagonal rows of *parang rusak* and *kawung* patterns. The presence of these once restricted court patterns makes one wonder if the figures on the other half of the *kain,* in their European uniforms, were not soldiers and officers of the Jogjakarta court, stepping out on parade. The arms (rifles and sabers?), the cannons, and the horses were all part of court paraphernalia. The usual orderly arrangement of central Javanese batiks seems to be forgotten here with the disappearance of truncated figures into the top border, and the organic transition between the figures and the geometric patterns. The foliate *tumpal* end panels introduce a stylistic element usually associated with the north coast. Compared with the other Jogjakarta pieces illustrated here, the quality of the workmanship appears much less precise, which suggests this piece was not made for court use.

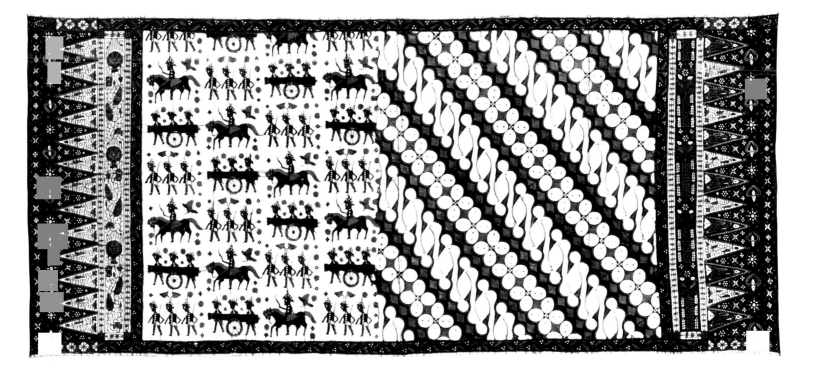

38

Sarong (skirt cloth)
Java
Batik
Cotton
Warp: 191.1 cm.; weft: 105.1 cm.
Los Angeles County Museum of Art
Costume Council Fund
M.77.71.8

Bold, austere striping entirely covers this unusual sarong. The diagonal movement of the *garis miring,* or slant line arrangement, is abruptly arrested by the horizontal striping of the *kepala.* The motifs filling the stripes have a structured, hard-edged quality intensified by the stark white ground. The spare use of a rust yellow slightly softens the strong blue and black. The geometric patterns such as *ceplok* and *tambal* ("patch"), used here as filling motifs, also occur on other batiks as the major motif.

39

Slendang (shoulder cloth)
Central Java
Batik
Cotton
Warp: 249 cm.; weft: 50.9 cm.
Los Angeles County Museum of Art
Mr. and Mrs. Clarence Dixon
CR.52.61.6

Within the surface network of leafy tendrils that composes the classical *semen* pattern of this central Javanese *slendang* lies one of the richest configurations of symbols in all Javanese batik—that of a cosmic or sacred "landscape." The essential elements include hierarchically arranged mountains suggesting the cosmic mountain, Meru. When they occur in groups of three, they may have a tripartite plant form filling them from below. The plant may combine aspects of a tree, which may be the tree of life, and of a lotus with its complex rootstock. Together, the tree and lotus seem to symbolize fertility. Flanking the mountains are sanctuaries or shrines—places for meditation to accrue magical power or to seek divine revelation. *Garuda,* the celestial eagle, and other birds represent the aerial realm, the location of the cosmic mountain. Deer, or buffalo, with tendrils sprouting from their mouths represent the power of the earth's fertile growth. Together these elements suggest a macrocosm. Aspects of this theme also appear in the "garden landscapes" of some Cirebon batiks and in the gold-leaf glue work on the special blue and white *dodot bangun tulak* of central Java.

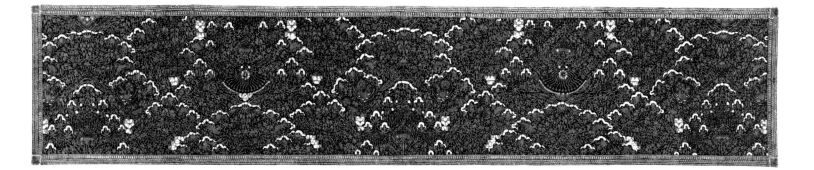

Bronwen and Garrett Solyom

The Balinese surround themselves with an extraordinary diversity of textiles with which they clothe not only their bodies but also the places and objects of great importance to them. This lavish use of cloth arises primarily from their religion, a unique interpretation of Hinduism that imposes powerful obligations on each individual and community to invoke the blessings of the gods, to honor the ancestors, and to propitiate the forces of evil at each step through life. The ceremonies required to achieve these ends range from simple daily offerings to extremely elaborate temple festivals. Most of them involve cloth in some way; as dress for the participants (the style of costume allowing for the display of several textiles at once); as honorific embellishment for the surrounding buildings, sculptures, and altars; or as the medium for certain magic powers.

For their ceremonies the Balinese expend a great deal of time in preparation. There seems to be both a delight in display and a strong sense of competition. Richness in dress, grace in movement, and artistry of expression are ideals, the signs of respectful attitudes toward the gods and ancestors. Within this context all the arts flourish and even the poorest villagers succeed in creating something elegant from less than splendid materials.[1] In seeking to fulfill these ideals the Balinese have been rather eclectic, quickly responding to new ideas and techniques, ingeniously adapting them to their own use.

These very general observations may partially explain the diversity of textile techniques found in Bali, the preference for richness and accents of brilliant color, and the variety of styles and combinations in which textiles are worn. There are many types of cloth, and each has many uses. At a temple festival, for example, one might observe the priest clad in white. The stone guardians at the gates might be draped with black and white check skirt cloths. The participants might wear striped, batik, or weft ikat underskirts with brilliant brocade sashes and breast cloths; the dancers might wear multicolored silks with gold-leaf glue work and elaborate headdresses of gilded carved leather. A neat stack of cloths of several kinds might rest among the offerings before the altar. Certain ceremonies or performances call for identical costumes but otherwise there is little uniformity, with everyone wearing the richest or best that he can afford or borrow.

Weaving is one of the basic activities of women and girls. Except for looms used to weave cloths with a continuous warp (see *geringsing,* below), most of the looms used in Bali are of the shed-stick and heddle type, in which the warp is stretched by means of a wooden hip yoke used as a backstrap. A band loom is also known.[2] While weaving is still done for family needs, since the 1960s it has become commercialized to supply the tourist market, usually with synthetic weft ikats for sarongs and inferior brocades.

In addition to textiles made in Bali, some are imported; Javanese batik, for example, is very widely used. Balinese everyday dress is relatively simple,[3] and Javanese batik skirt cloths are frequently part of it, especially for the women. They may also be worn ceremonially by both men and women. *Lokcan,* the Javanese silk *slendang,* appear as part of ceremonial costume: as breast cloths, waist sashes, skirts, and overskirts, or draped over the shoulder. It is curious that although batik is so common, the process does not seem to have been practiced in Bali,[4] whereas other resist techniques, *plangi* and *tritik,* are known. Since communications with nearby Java have been relatively open, it has probably been easier to import batik than to make it.

White cloth: In the hierarchy of textiles, plain white cloth is very important, for as a symbol of purity it has many roles. For festivals the temple facade may be hung with it. Pennants *(penyor),* said to be symbols of the sacred mountain Agung, and ceremonial umbrellas carried in processions may also be made of it. Priestly garments are basically white. Participants in very serious ceremonies such as obtaining holy water or attending the bathing of the gods in the sea may wrap themselves in white, covering their bright brocade skirts. At cremations, white cloth is everywhere. White headbands distinguish the mourners, for example, and the corpse is wrapped in many yards of white, some of it covered with special symbols drawn by the priest to assist the soul in entering heaven.[5] After the corpse is burned, the cremation pavilion is closed off with a rope of white yarn "to forget the dead."[6] White cloth also appears as the dress of dancers; for example, *keris* dancers may use it for their loincloths. These dancers represent the forces of good against the evil witch, Rangda. In her hands a special white cloth becomes a magical weapon with powers to defeat her attackers, make her invisible, etc. In contrast to white cloth, black cloth is sometimes associated with the unclean; a black skirt cloth, for example, may be worn by menstruating women.[7]

Poleng: Color symbolism in Bali is very complex. Another holy, magically powerful cloth is *poleng,* a black and white check that perhaps symbolizes the dualism of fertility and death, white and black magic, as well as positive versus negative, good versus evil.[8] It is found in many contexts: draping the stone figures guarding doorways and gates, as costume in sacred dances, on the drums of the *gamelan* (an ensemble of traditional musical instruments), as overskirts or coats for priests. It appears to serve a protective function, keeping away evil spirits. A very ancient motif, it is worn by several of the characters of the *wayang* epics. Possibly the motif harks back to the patchwork coats of rags traditionally worn by Buddhist priests, and, if so, has a strong possible association with Javanese batiks with *tambal* (patch) patterns. Sometimes *poleng* has three colors—white, red, and black—which may represent the trinity of Siva, Brahma, Vishnu.[9]

The three-color *poleng* is the simplest of all motifs found on *geringsing*.

Supplementary weft: Patterning with weft brocade, often loosely referred to as *songket,* is perhaps the most common method of ornamenting ceremonial garments for dance and for rituals (see no. 40). It displays the widest variety of colors in the boldest combinations of any Balinese textile. The ground is usually plain-colored silk (or perhaps a synthetic), although woven stripes and plaids are also found. Stiff gold and silver metallic gimp, either alone or combined with plain-colored cotton or silk yarns, forms the pattern. Popular motifs include flowers, either as isolated small ornaments in a center field surrounded by a wide elaborate border or as larger, strongly textured allover patterns that have become more stylized. Other purely geometric motifs include brocade versions of *tambal, ceplok,* or zigzags. Occasionally, bright bands of weft ikat introduce a subtle counterpoint to shining metallic yarns, especially in cloths with an allover laddered or structured triangular pattern. The least common but the most spectacular are figural motifs: large masks, statuesque animals, formal *wayang* scenes. The town of Klungkung is particularly famous for its brocades.

Supplementary warp: There are some isolated examples of an unusual supplementary warp technique occurring on Bali. All that is known of their exact provenance is the field observation by Christian Pelras that some were made near Kesiman outside Denpasar.[10] They bear a striking resemblance to the rectangular palm leaf ornaments, *lamak,* which are hung as decoration from temple and house altars on feast days, and probably serve the same ritual function. Usually these woven *lamak* have severe geometric patterning and in the central part there appears to be a *cili,* a female figure usually connected with Devi Sri, goddess of rice and agriculture.

Prada: The application of gold to the surface of a cloth is a popular decorative technique, producing textiles known as *kain prada.* Traditionally, gold leaf or dust was glued to the fabric; today, in many cases, gold-colored paint is substituted.[11] When applied to Javanese batik, the gold either follows the batik pattern—for example, geometric motifs such as *kawung* or *ceplok*—or may introduce a different pattern entirely. More often, plain-colored silks or cottons are used (and probably synthetics as well). They are bright red, purple, green, yellow, or black, or sometimes two or three colors combined. The *prada* motifs reflect some of the ornamental richness of Bali's stone temple reliefs. They include stylized lotus flowers or meanders, regularly repeated or more freely arranged and incorporating leaves and tendrils. *Banji* (swastikas), Chinese cloud patterns, and foliate *tumpal* are found in the borders. Animals such as the *singha* (lion), bull, phoenix, and peacock also occur. At their best, *kain prada* are bold and sumptuous, although at times they may be overwhelmingly gaudy.

They are sometimes worn by wedding couples or hung from altars or even from tall offering structures. Their most effective use is, however, for theatrical costumes. Made in many sizes, from narrow bands to full width skirt cloths, they may be hung, draped, or tightly wound round the body, and when the music begins, they flash and shimmer with the movement of the dance.

Plangi: Tie-dyed textiles, usually sashes, continue to be made in Bali today, although the patterns are simple and show little variation. They are usually squares filled with a flower form or a large lozenge on red, green, or purple grounds with other bright colors painted into the outlined shapes.[12] This technique is known from both north and south Bali. Combinations of *plangi* with *tritik,* or stitch resist, occur, but only infrequently.[13] Silk is the preferred material, although synthetics are apparently also used. The patterns recall *patola* but are "so simple that Indian influence cannot be claimed with certainty."[14] As with other Balinese textiles, *plangi* pieces are worn in many ways by both men and women, wrapped as breast cloths, waist sashes, or overskirts.

Weft ikat: This technique occurs in both north and south Bali. Excluding the contemporary commercial ikat sarongs, there appear to be several distinct traditions. In south Bali, and also the nearby island of Nusa Penida, sturdy cotton ikats are made in red, blue, and white. After the red dyeing, the blue and sometimes small areas of different colors may be directly applied to the yarns with bamboo sticks. Both in the division into side and end borders and in the center-field patterns they recall *patola.*[15] Silk weft ikats also occur quite widely in Bali, with a variety of designs ranging from simply placed flower sprays to busy geometric patterns, the latter also sometimes reminiscent of *patola.* They are frequently worn as skirt cloths. Distinctive polychrome silk weft ikats with *wayang* figures occur as well. In some, scenes from the shadow plays are recreated with full feeling; in others, less successful figures stand stiffly in confronting pairs. They may be further ornamented with brocaded end panels. There is also one special group of figural weft ikats in silk that distinctly imitates one of the figural patterns of the Balinese double ikat, *geringsing.*

Geringsing: More than any other cloth in Bali, the cotton double-ikat *geringsing* made only in the village of Tenganan Pegeringsingan are linked with ritual. From the time the yarns are first measured out to the moment the cloth is worn out or sold outside the village, each *geringsing* is subject to the prescriptions of *adat.* The painstakingly complex process of measuring out both warp and weft yarns, binding, and dyeing them prior to weaving has been described elsewhere.[16] It should be noted that it may take years for a *geringsing* to be finished, more because of ritual requirements, such as waiting for an auspicious day to work, than the actual hours of work involved. The yarns are dyed two colors. Indigo dyeing is done outside the village, then the yarns are returned for the longer process of steeping in the rust red. This red, sometimes dyed over the blue, gives the cloths their distinctive deep purple brown and red hues. There is some debate whether a token amount of human blood was ever a ritual ingredient in the red dye.[17] There are many enigmas about *geringsing,* and the problem of how the double-ikat technique came to be practiced in only one village in all of Indonesia may never be satisfactorily resolved. The cloths with geometric-floral motifs suggest some connections with *patola,* while those with *wayang* figures show similarities with figures on thirteenth-century east Javanese temple reliefs (see no. 43). *Geringsing* with square patterns *(poleng)* may also relate to old Javanese patterns. The repertoire of motifs is relatively small and very conservative; the patterns have not changed much. The only variations seem to arise from the ways two or more patterns may be combined in one cloth (see no. 42).

There are several sizes of *geringsing* and they are used within the village in various ways.[18] Since they are woven with a continuous warp, they come off the loom with the fringes uncut. Some are stored by the village in this state and may be loaned to individuals for offering purposes. With the fringes cut, they are used as clothing for ritual occasions. Specific combinations of cloths identify the wearers with particular groups within the village. For death rituals a *geringsing* is used to cover the genitals of a deceased person, and thereafter becomes unclean. It is then sold outside the village, as are new ones in which the dyeing is imperfect. Other Balinese greatly value *geringsing* for the powers attributed to them: healing, protection against evil, and transmission of magical strength.[19] The name *geringsing* is frequently translated as "without sickness" from *gering,* "sick," and *sing,* "without." *Gering,* however, also refers more generally to evil spirits approaching from the direction of the sea.[20] Both the name of the cloths and of the village may therefore carry something of the meaning "without evil" or "pure."

Notes

1.
One of the best descriptions of Balinese dance costume is given by de Zoete and Spies, pp. 40-44. Many of their remarks apply to Balinese ceremonial costume in general.

2.
A valuable discussion of Balinese looms is given by Bolland, pp. 171-82. See also Covarrubias, pp. 100-101.

3.
Covarrubias (pp. 109-11) describes the everyday dress of men and women. His observations made in the 1930s still apply today, except perhaps for the increasing popularity of Western dress and the decreasing frequency with which men and women wear nothing above the waist. See also Pelras, 1962, pp. 216-18.

4.
Covarrubias (p. 199) notes "strange batiks in a rough hand woven cotton of non-Javanese style" but could not discover if they were made in Bali. Pelras (1962, p. 232) also notes an atelier in the region of Karangasem making batiks in 1962.

5.
Covarrubias, pp. 365 and 368. He also mentions that the priest writes inscriptions on "little pieces of a sort of tapa from the Celebes, a specially prescribed paper made of beaten tree-bark."

6.
Ibid., p. 377.

7.
Mershon, p. 122.

8.
J. L. Swellengrebel, introduction to *Bali: Studies in Life, Thought and Ritual.* The Hague: W. van Hoeve, 1960, pp. 40 and 107.

9.
Ibid., p. 45.

10.
Pelras, 1967, p. 259. For a further discussion, see Langewis, 1956, pp. 31-47.

11.
Maxwell and Maxwell, p. 11.

12.
Thelma R. Newman, *Contemporary Southeast Asian Arts and Crafts.* New York: Crown, 1977, pp. 37-39.

13.
Alfred Bühler, "Plangi—The Tie and Dye Work," *Ciba Review,* no. 104, 1954, p. 3740.

14.
Bühler, 1959, p. 18.

15.
Ibid., p. 41.

16.
Bühler, Ramseyer, and Ramseyer-Gygi, pp. 59-64. Also, Larsen, Bühler, Solyom, and Solyom, pp. 222-27.

17.
Katharane Mershon (p. 19) makes one of the more sober observations on this subject. "The practice of drawing blood from aged persons who are near death was considered a communal rite, and therefore garments dyed through such a procedure had great essential value, enriching communal welfare."

18.
A recent account of use is given in Bühler, Ramseyer, and Ramseyer-Gygi, pp. 53-55.

19.
For examples of use of *geringsing* outside Tenganan, see Covarrubias, pp. 24, 153, 231; de Zoete and Spies, pp. 91, 112-13; Jasper and Pirngadie, 1912, p. 290; and Korn, p. 314.

20.
Jane Belo, *Trance in Bali.* New York: Columbia University Press, 1960, p. 199.

40

Kain Songket (skirt cloth), detail
Bali
Supplementary weft on plain weave
Silk, gold and silver metallic-wrapped
yarns
Warp: 184 cm.; weft: 134.7 cm.
Los Angeles County Museum of Art
Costume Council and Museum
Associates Purchase
M.77.90.1

In this unusual weft brocade an angular, small-scale pattern is executed in gold and silver paper-backed metallic yarns on a plain woven silk ground. Broad longitudinal stripes are composed of repeating pattern units that camouflage abstracted birds and animals fused with geometric forms. The pattern is intercepted by two bands of lozenges and foliate *tumpal* motifs that span the cloth. This division of the cloth suggests a *kepala,* although the main pattern is continued between the bands. The end borders are finished with the same lozenge motifs halved into triangles. The two identical panels of the cloth are joined along the selvage, forming a rectangular garment that was possibly worn ceremonially as a skirt cloth or overskirt.

Only traces of gold and silver remain on the supplementary metallic yarns; they are so worn that the cloth, in the deep rich red favored for many Balinese textiles, has acquired a muted character. These metallic yarns, in three distinct colors and thicknesses, were systematically and sensitively manipulated to form pattern elements of alternating value.

41

Slendang (shoulder cloth)
Bali
Weft brocade and weft ikat on plain weave
Silk, gold and silver metallic-wrapped yarns
Warp: 189.2 cm.; weft: 48.9 cm.
Los Angeles County Museum of Art
Costume Council Fund
M.73.105

This nineteenth-century (?) silk weft brocade also has a plain weave red silk ground with patterning in gold and silver paper-backed metallic yarns. It illustrates another characteristic favored in some Balinese textiles: the use of bright polychrome silk to accentuate motifs. In the center field the regular zigzag pattern is enlivened by the apparently random arrangement of bright colors, now partially worn away, that once completely filled the longitudinal bands. The end panels contain several discrete motifs, loosely grouped but not quite symmetrically placed. The orientation of these motifs, perpendicular to the weft, suggests that the cloth would be hung or worn vertically.

Heads (or masks) without bodies occur occasionally on Balinese brocades and ikats. Here the lions' heads with flamelike manes and pendant tongues symbolize a guardian function, as they sometimes do in Bali today, especially in sculpture. Another important motif on the end panels is the *cakra,* a symbolic four-spoked wheel. The attribute and magical weapon of the god Vishnu, it is also found on amulets protecting against witches.[1] The presence of both the *cakra* and the lion strongly suggests a ritual protective role for the whole cloth.

1.
Covarrubias, p. 346.

42

Kain Geringsing (shoulder cloth)
Tenganan, Bali
Embroidery and double ikat on plain weave
Cotton, gold and silver metallic-wrapped yarns
Warp: 203.3 cm.; weft: 50.2 cm.
Los Angeles County Museum of Art
Costume Council Fund
M.75.8
(See color plate, p. 18)

One aspect of the technical sophistication of Balinese double ikat is the frequency with which one standard pattern may be either obviously combined or more subtly merged with another. In this floral-geometric *geringsing* the center section of the pattern field exemplifies the *cemplong* pattern with white schematized blossoms, which are possibly lotuses.[1] Toward the selvages, however, the blossoms alternate with deep red hooked ovals that appear to be taken from the *enjekan siap* pattern. This subtle manipulation of two patterns increases the interest of the cloth. The embroidery added at each end in gold and silver metallic paper-backed yarns is a more obvious elaboration. Now somewhat worn, the yarns generally follow and conceal the dyed pattern of the end borders and partially cover the dyed center-field patterns.

1.
Bühler, Ramseyer, and Ramseyer-Gygi, p. 70, fig. 53.

43

Kain Geringsing (shoulder cloth)
Tenganan, Bali
Embroidery and double ikat on plain
weave
Cotton, gold and silver metallic-
wrapped yarns
Warp: 209.6 cm.; weft: 53.3 cm.
Mary Kefgen
EX.77.249

Clearly this is one of the most dis-
tinctively and lavishly embroidered
geringsing of the *wayang kebo* pattern. The center field, dominated
by a single four-pointed star form,
consists of four flattened half-
ellipses. Each contains two scenes,
separated by a plant form, with
three human figures in each. The
figures, dyed purple red, are sil-
houetted against the white resisted
ground. The endmost portions
of four of the scenes are eclipsed
by the abstract angular branching
of heavily textured silver
yarn that is embroidered across the
end panels and onto the center
field. Executed with a careful hand,
the embroidery stitches cover the
white resisted ground so that the

purple red of the figures becomes
the background for the silver. The
postures of the three figures
suggest an "audience scene," with
one kneeling to pay obeisance to
the other two seated figures. Possibly related to east Javanese temple
reliefs, the scene displays a timeless
formal quality, the figures frozen in
attitude and gesture. Photographs
show similar pieces with apparently
less embroidery worn as shoulder
cloths by young girls performing
the *rejang* dance in Tenganan.[1]

1.
Bühler, Ramseyer, and Ramseyer-
Gygi, pl. 31.

Sumba

Steven G. Alpert

In Sumba, as in other areas of Indonesia, weaving is a jealously guarded activity of women. The manufacture of fine textiles was traditionally the exclusive right of high-ranking women, but now any woman may weave them. Nevertheless, most of the textiles produced by the Sumbanese for their own use are still tied or woven at the request of persons of high social rank.[1] Superior weaving is an arduous process that requires total concentration; one piece may take months or even years to complete. Since the secret of a fine ikat lies in tightly wrapping the warp threads, a weaver can produce precious cloths only as long as her eyes remain strong and her fingers pliant. Therefore, girls begin at a very young age to help collect plant dyes, prepare and spin cotton, and learn the rudiments of the ikat and supplementary weft processes. By the time they have reached their late teens they display a virtuosity on the loom.

Sumbanese women are unusually prolific weavers, meeting a constant demand for both ritual and commercial cloth. A wide range of textiles are manufactured on Sumba; the three most important types are represented here.

Hinggi: Large blankets always woven in pairs—one piece worn as a waist garment or sarong, the other draped over the shoulder (see no. 44). Designs include large geometric patterns and organic forms woven using the ikat technique. Now worn by men as festive garb, they also serve as shrouds. The best pieces are still reserved for nobility. Finishing bands, or *kabakil,* are added by supplementary warp weaving and show that a particular blanket has been "brought to life" and is ready to be worn. Fine *hinggi* are frequently referred to as *kain raja*—that is, those blankets that are of raja status—or given specific endearing names referring to one or more outstanding characteristic. *Hinggi kombu* (see nos. 45, 46) feature a rust to deep red color—*kombu,* derived from the *mengkudu* tree—as well as indigo and occasionally a tan yellow stain that is applied after weaving.

Lau pahudu: Women's sarongs or ceremonial waist garments banded with geometric patterns or with rows of repeated animal or human figures using the supplementary warp technique. *Lau pahudu padua* combine both the supplementary technique with ikat sections in *kombu* or other tones. Other features of traditional *lau* might include stained design highlights; a fringe *(wonogiri)* on which trade beads might be strung; or a *katipa,* a narrow beaded strand. Like the *hinggi,* fine quality *lau* are reserved for the nobility.

Lau hada: Women's waist garments using old trade beads and *nassa* shells to depict an unusual variety of fanciful animals or human characters (see no. 47). Now rare, such *lau* are associated with the highest rank of nobility and with funeral rites.[2]

Over the centuries images of power and status have been assimilated from foreign sources into the weaver's repertoire. Chinese traders searching for sandalwood during the later Sung and Yüan dynasties brought porcelain, cloth, and precious metals. The exuberant *nagas,* or dragons, that grace many Sumbanese weavings are descended from the celadon ceramics of that period. The center sections of many *hinggi* and the decorated bands of many royal *lau* display intricate geometric designs called *patola ratu,* which are associated with Indian *patola* cloth. Reputed to have great magical power, *patola* are among the most sacred of objects and, like porcelains, are carefully stored in double-storied "royal treasuries" or *adat* houses. Rende cloths dating from the 1920s and 1930s, brought to Rende by Arab traders, often depict the curious winged horse that Mohammed rode on his flight into the desert in 622 A.D., a motif reflecting the influence of Arab trade. On other Sumbanese textiles, lions—some fierce and others playful—eye each other in a familiar balanced composition borrowed from the coats of arms on European silver coins.

All along the east coast of the island *hinggi* and *lau* serve as principal articles of exchange, making them an important factor in Sumba's economy. Cloth is usually not sold on the open market, but exchanged with other districts through a system of familial ties and inheritance. The exchange takes place as part of a system of favors granted, for example, in times of need or in recognition of ritual obligations. Since every event of passage, every crisis, is recorded by the transfer of gifts that include *kain* there is a constant circulation of ritual items and wealth. The use and dispensation of fine textiles has traditionally been the privilege of the nobility, who out of generosity or a desire to enhance their status would lend or give cloth to retainers on ceremonial occasions. Royalty had the right to demand any textile from a follower at any time. Death was the customary penalty for those who broke the proscriptions surrounding the manufacture and use of textiles, and even now certain royal patterns and dye combinations remain closely guarded community secrets.

According to the Sumbanese, harmony is achieved by balancing the male and female principles, and this concept regulates the exchange of gifts, which are classified as "male" or "female." In marriage, the bride's family would be expected to supply not only male and female *kain,* but also porcelain, beads, and sacrificial animals. The male's kin would produce dowry items made of precious metals—earrings, necklaces, and weapons—as well as horses, sacrificial animals, and perhaps slaves. Marriage without such gift exchanges would be inconceivable for the Sumbanese. Gift exchanges also take place whenever royalty meet on ceremonial occasions. Fine cloth is still presented to esteemed foreign guests or to those who have witnessed an important ceremony as a token of their participation and a bond of friendship.

The system of gift exchange and the use of textiles is nowhere so elaborate as in royal funerals. The dressed and bejeweled corpse is wrapped in what can be an enormous quantity of blankets: a raja might be wrapped in as many as one hundred or more individual *hinggi.* The corpse might remain for a number of months or years after the primary burial ceremonies before the final burial can be arranged. The manpower and the drain of wealth involved at this time are enormous for the family of the deceased, for it is they who must call all the related clans to witness the ceremony. Although these visitors do bring gifts of *kain* and precious metal, the host family is required to slaughter animals daily, to house and feed the royal parties until their resources are nearly exhausted. Roos, an early visitor to Sumba, describes the burial of the ruler of Melolo when a prince and his entourage literally ate up everything.[3]

Most of the textiles that a raja amasses during his lifetime are expected to be buried with him, an essential part of the goods he will require in the next life. Textiles of superior quality are therefore seldom worn or even displayed. They are carefully hoarded in large wooden chests or in covered baskets made of woven *lontar* leaves that hang from the house rafters, waiting to be buried along with a vast quantity of other grave goods. Formerly, favorite animals such as horses or hunting dogs were ceremonially wounded and left to die on the burial plain; slaves were sacrificed; and large stone monuments were erected as memorials to a dying lord.

The Sumbanese weaver could use only certain motifs, but was free to organize them however she liked. Repetitive bands or large open areas swarm with animal, avian, and aquatic creatures. Stylized human figures appear engaged in a variety of activities: ritual dancing; horseback riding; victory celebrations around the *pohon andung,* or skull tree, that once marked every royal village. Behind such groups loom the outlines of ancestors, shadowy faces and figures somewhere between the forces of the visible and invisible.[4] These are not unlike Marapu, the great spirits or deities with innumerable forms and faces that inhabit every aspect of the Sumbanese world. Fine old *hinggi kombu* present strikingly familiar images from daily life combined with a more subtle sense of the Sumbanese metaphysical world. This duality between conscious and unconscious design translates into great aesthetic tension that has produced textiles of magnificent depth and mystery.

Now, however, as the carefully defined traditions of *adat* have broken down, the identity of many individual motifs and combined patterns has been lost, and designs from various districts have been combined in a seemingly random fashion. Sumbanese textiles from the late nineteenth and early twentieth centuries are vigorous and traditional, with deep tones and fine finish. But by the 1920s imported thread and synthetic dyes had become more common, which allowed the weaver to expand her production considerably as the first tourists, colonial administrators, and traders

began to buy Sumbanese textiles as colorful curios. Fewer fine textiles were woven as the demands for an ever increasing commercial market were met. Today a large colony of immigrants from neighboring islands, principally Savu and Flores, also engage in weaving quick commercial Sumbanese cloth that bears little resemblance to the traditional models.

A Sumbanese woman removes some of the bast ties from an ikat warp. At this point, the warp has already been tied once and submerged in the dye (probably blue). All the areas that now appear white had been completely covered with ties. The warps will probably be tied again in preparation for the second, or red, dye.

Notes

1.
Personal communication, Tamu Umbu
W. Tanangoendjoe, Uma Bara, Raja of
Melolo, East Sumba, July 1977.

2.
Most of the information contained in
this article has been obtained during
my visits to Sumba over the past eight
years. Much of this material has been
published by Marie Jeanne Adams in
her many excellent articles listed in the
bibliography. I have used her thorough
"System and Meaning in East Sumba
Textile Design: A Study in Traditional
Art," as a constant reference when preparing this article.

3.
S. Roos, "Beschryving van voorwerpen
afkomstig van Soemba, aan het Ethnologische Museum (Batavia), aangeboden
door S. Roos, *Notulen van de Algemeene
en Directievergaderingen van het Bataviaasch genootschap van kunsten en
wetenschappen,* vol. 9, 1872, p. 41.

4.
Personal communication, Tamu Umbu
W. Tanangoendjoe, Uma Bara, Raja of
Melolo, East Sumba, March 1977.

Hinggi (man's shawl or waist cloth)
Kenatan, East Sumba
Warp ikat
Cotton
Warp: 243.8 cm.; weft: 124.4 cm.
Steven G. Alpert
EX.77.239

Certain features mark this example
as a classic *hinggi*: the choice of
symbols and their elegant distribution, the yellow color, and the fine
kabakil end borders with corded
fringe. The cockatoo and *patola*
motifs are both aristocratic symbols, and the omega-shaped motif
in the central band is a symbol of
the ancient gold *mamuli,* or ear ornament, that is a traditional marriage gift. The yellow color, applied
after the *hinggi* is woven, is a re-
mainder from an older tradition of
gilding the fabrics. MHK

Hinggi Kombu (man's shawl or waist cloth)
Melolo-Rende (?), East Sumba
Warp ikat
Cotton
Warp: 248.9 cm.; weft: 120.6 cm.
Los Angeles County Museum of Art
Costume Council Fund
M.74.19.2

The highest ranked ikat shawls in Sumba are called *hinggi kombu.* They feature abstract designs and a deep rust color produced by the very complex *kombu* dye process, which requires the use of plant oils; plants containing alum, which serves as a mordant; and dye obtained from *mengkudu* roots. The bright red rust color of this cloth appears especially rich against the narrow white design bands and the bold dark central section. The *kabakil* with supplementary yarns depicting birds at rest is very finely woven. Such borders are woven onto the shawl after the two major panels have been completed and joined. The striped ikatted warp yarns for the *kabakil* are set close together on a small narrow belt-type loom, and small groups of unwoven warp ends from the large blanket become the weft of the border. MJL

46

Hinggi Kombu (man's shawl or waist cloth)
Sumba, east end section
Warp ikat
Cotton
Warp: 254 cm.; weft: 111.8 cm.
Los Angeles County Museum of Art
Costume Council Fund
M.74.19.1

A handsome and unusual aspect of this *hinggi* is the shift in design at the center of the cloth. This *pagi-sore* effect may have been inspired by batik sarong designs imported from Java. Motifs on recent *hinggi* are often freely adapted from various districts of Sumba as well as from foreign sources; here, for example, the paired lions holding a scepter were borrowed from the coat of arms on old Dutch coins. The significance of the letter forms woven into the *kabakil* is not known. The female forms with arms akimbo, the stylized animals, and the *patola*-inspired center band are all traditional *hinggi* designs.

MJL

47
Lau Hada (woman's skirt cloth)
East Sumba
Plain weave, appliqué
Cotton, trade beads, shells
Warp: 119.4 cm.; weft: 73.7 cm.
Indianapolis Museum of Art
EX.77.289
(See color plate, p. 19)

48
Breast Ornament
Rendi, East Sumba
Net beading
Cotton, glass trade beads
Warp: 39.4 cm.; width: 23.5 cm.
Los Angeles County Museum of Art
Costume Council Fund
M.77.91.2b

Skirts decorated with beads and shells—*lau hada*—are part of the costume worn by noblewomen at funeral ceremonies for royalty. Monumental in design and symbolism, the cloth serves a symbolic protective function. Its name describes it as a "screen against the moon and a protection against the sun."[1] The orant human figures guide the soul to the other world, while the shrimp suggest the dangers of travel from earth to the new world by their own vulnerability in the time between shedding the old shell and growing a new one.[2]   MJL

1.
Adams, 1969, p. 166.
2.
Ibid., p. 167.

Beaded ornaments of this type are worn around the neck as part of the traditional funerary garb (see no. 47). The horses portrayed here may serve as symbolic mounts for passage into the spiritual world.[1]   MJL

1.
Adams, 1969, p. 167.

49

Lau (woman's skirt cloth)
Pao, East Sumba
Supplementary warp on plain weave,
warp ikat, appliqué
Cotton, glass beads
Warp: 132.1 cm.; weft: 162.6 cm.
Los Angeles County Museum of Art
Costume Council Fund
M.77.20.1

An elaborate old *katipa* (beaded
band) filled with flowing bird and
snake motifs graces this *lau* from
the late 1940s. Commercially dyed
yarns have been used except in the
kombu ikat areas. The major decorative band of supplementary warp
features a traditional *patola ratu*
(royal) pattern.   MHK

Kent Watters

Flores, known locally as Nusa Bunga (Flower Island), is a long, narrow island in the center of the Lesser Sunda chain. A series of magnificent volcanoes runs east to west along the rugged island; high forested ridges and deep winding gorges end abruptly in the rocky bluffs of the south coast. The north coast, by contrast, is barren, with rolling hills and arid brushland.

Flores is inhabited by numerous distinct ethnic groups, each with its own language, tribal customs, and unique textiles. Undoubtedly the ruggedness of the terrain has been a major factor in preserving this ethnic autonomy. Much of the cultural foundation of these various groups can be attributed to the megalithic and Dongson periods, and Flores is often included with Sumatra, Borneo, Celebes, and Sumba as one of the few places still containing much evidence of these early migrations. Stone megaliths, certain decorative designs, and skills such as ikat weaving are typical reminders of these earlier cultures. Previously, tribal warfare and head-hunting were also part of the *adat* in Flores, but the mass conversion to Catholicism which began in the 1920s ended this particular aspect of *adat* and culturally neutralized most of the indigenous ethnic groups. Today, with five bishops and scores of missionaries firmly entrenched, Flores is a bastion of Catholicism in Indonesia. Some traditional customs and animistic rituals survive, but compared to the colorful "pagan" lifestyles still found in Sumba and Borneo, Flores is culturally barren. The weaving of fine ikats is one of the few traditional cultural expressions still surviving.

The people of Flores present an intriguing blend of Proto-Malay, Melanesian, and Papuan traits. Occasionally, Portuguese racial features and surnames appear in coastal villages used as trading ports four hundred years ago. Farming occupies most of a man's life; fishing and hunting are minimal. Women occasionally help in the fields, but usually they are occupied at home with domestic chores. In some areas the women spend most of their time weaving, while their other activities are minimal; in other areas no weaving is done at all. In general, however, the women of Flores are prolific weavers who work daily from early womanhood until their eyesight becomes too poor in old age to continue. Their textiles vary from the simplest, coarsest cloth to some of the finest, most sophisticated in Indonesia.

The far western end of Flores is inhabited by the Manggarai people, who wear handspun cotton sarongs dyed a blue black indigo (see no. 54). A narrow, vertical panel of multicolored geometric and rosette patterns woven in the *songket* technique is generally the only decoration, although occasionally the sarongs are ornamented with similar motifs individually spaced over the body of the cloth. Black sarongs are worn by most men of Flores, although decorative techniques vary from group to group.

Moving east from Manggarai through the lush, cold mountainous areas of central Flores, one descends eventually into the land of the Nage-Keo, situated around the town of Baowai. The Nage-Keo women still weave the traditional woman's *adat* sarong and man's shawl. Both are made from coarse, heavy handspun cotton thread colored with natural dyes. The patterns are simple dots, dashes, and sometimes florals, always warp ikatted in white on blue or red bands. The sarongs form part of a young woman's dowry and are worn only during special ceremonies, while the shawls are worn by the men to complete their costume on any special occasion.

East of Nage-Keo in central Flores lies the Lio kingdom, stretching 100 kilometers east to west and touching both coasts. Many generations ago the region was divided among the three sons of a dying king. One area was given the exclusive right to produce pottery; another was allocated the weaving of mats and baskets; and the third became the center of woven textiles. Intended to promote peaceful, cooperative interaction, this subdivision was successful and is still adhered to today. A side effect of the split, however, was the eventual breakdown of a unified region into numerous autonomous villages. Not until the early twentieth century was the whole area again united under one leader and given the name Lio.

The textile region consists of a few main villages and some smaller ones scattered through the mountains. Since the women must supply the rest of the kingdom with textiles they spend most of their time weaving. Generally the sarongs made for personal use are of higher quality than the commercial ones made to be sold at the small village markets, although sometimes weavers will accept commissions to make better sarongs for special customers. The high demand for sarongs has been a major factor in discontinuing the use of natural, local materials for dyeing and weaving. Today virtually all commercial sarongs are made with imported synthetic dyes and rayon threads.

The production of ikat textiles occupies most of a woman's day. After the morning coffee the husband leaves for the fields and the children go off to play. The wife retires to the front porch where she will spend the entire morning ikatting (tying off) a small section of white threads stretched on a frame. The ikatting of threads for a single sarong will require weeks or even months to complete, depending on the design and how often the woman works. Betel nuts, considered a necessary stimulant, are always close at hand.

Often a weaver will work on several sarongs simultaneously. If she becomes weary with the ikatting of one piece, she may put it aside and go to one of the special areas in the village reserved for dyeing, where she will dye the threads for another sarong. The preparation of dyes and the dyeing of threads with traditional, natural materials is a daily ritual lasting for months. Indigo leaves must ferment for days and then be mixed with lime and ash-water in a series of pots before the blue dye is ready. The bark of *kombu* roots must be pounded, chopped, and squeezed repeatedly in water before the dyeing of red brown can begin. Since up to sixty pounds of *kombu* roots are required to complete the dyeing for one sarong, there is a perpetual shortage of these roots. Often a weaver must wait until more roots can be dug without killing her trees, or she must purchase these and other special dye materials at high prices from neighboring areas.

It is easy to understand why most weavers today prefer simply to open a small packet of cheap imported synthetic dye and within a few days have brightly colored finished threads. Even Lio weavings meant for personal use now often rely heavily on synthetic materials. The reasons are not entirely economic, however, for often the traditional colors are referred to as *warna mati*, or "dead colors." Also, the fine traditional handspun cotton thread has been replaced by cotton and rayon trade thread because the people like the soft feel and lively sheen of the finished fabric.

Nevertheless, few of the synthetic ingredients can capture the unusual qualities of a traditional Lio weaving. In the finest pieces rich, subtle maroon brown tones seem to float through the body of the cloth. There is a warmth in these deep earth tones that uniquely characterizes Lio ikats. Sometimes they are ornamented with red and blue highlights that give additional life and color to the weaving. Unfortunately, only a few weavers still appreciate this and continue to make ikats in the traditional manner. These fine rare pieces are usually made to be kept and worn on special occasions.

The Lio woman's sarong is a narrow tube composed of three or four sections totaling nearly six feet in length (see no. 50). The two mirror-image end sections are decorated with a series of dark bands containing warp ikat designs; warp ikat motifs also decorate the dark background of the center piece(s). The women handle their sarongs constantly, pulling them over their shoulders, then over their heads, then unfolding and folding them again at the waist, always feeling and playing with the cloth. Their sarongs provide tangible comfort, warmth, and protection in an often harsh environment. But they do not save sarongs as heirlooms nor do they have special ceremonies for the making or wearing of these cloths. Some sarongs might be buried with the owner but this is not an *adat* custom. The women each have several pieces that they wear, and several that are kept folded up in a cupboard or chest. Generally they appreciate a sarong while the cloth lasts or until they need to sell it, and after that they simply wear another one.

Lio ikat designs consist of fine lines, usually white, light brown, or pale yellow. On more complicated pieces these lines outline areas of red or blue on a dark ground. The intricate geometrics of most Lio designs display a strong *patola* influence, although stick-figure people, lizards, and sacred earrings are sometimes portrayed. Large, bold ikat patterns such as those found in Celebes, Sumba, and other islands neighboring Flores are not found in Lio. The use of fine lines to form intricate designs in warp ikat is unique to Lio and to some Iban weaving in Borneo. This difficult and complicated ikat workmanship places these pieces on a superior technical level shared only with the weft ikat silks of Sumatra and Java. But more important than just technical expertise are the sensitivity and finesse expressed in the unique design work of Lio ikats.

Nearly all Lio sarongs are categorized and named according to overall composition. Each type has specific design elements that are always used in the same position within the piece. Occasionally there is a minor modification of design elements within the composition but the basic layout of each type remains the same. Often women will know the names of sarong types of which few or no actual examples survive. Since there are no design models or sample patterns, these types are lost forever unless an old woman can make one before she dies. Any meanings the names may once have had are now forgotten. There are no special designs for aristocracy despite the existence of a definite social hierarchy.

Some villages prefer certain sarong types over others, although most types are usually found in every village. The majority of pieces might fall into four or five named categories but the exact total number of categories is unknown: the author knows of at least ten and the people have said there are more. They know the names but finding examples can be extremely difficult. Although weavers are always free to create whatever compositions they choose, the majority prefer to reproduce the traditional types taught to them by their mothers or copied from existing pieces. Several sarong types are identified by the weavers as being the most traditional. These consist of blue and maroon brown bands ornamented only with white designs that are more Dongson in nature, consisting of simple zigzags, concentric diamond shapes, and exploding stars. These types probably predate the introduction of *patola* into the Lio area. There is also a special type of black, striped sarong, which consists of a heavy handspun cotton with beadwork designs ornamenting a band at the bottom. These are quite old and are used only in a rain dance during times of drought.

Some of the most interesting weavings are those rare pieces with imaginative compositions not found in the usual categories. Often the design elements are similar to those found in traditional compositions, but the overall pattern is unique and has no name. The weaver will ikat the designs directly from her imagination or vision without drawing them first. In fact, since ikat is their medium, many weavers cannot draw their designs accurately.

The Lio man's *adat* shawl, nearly an exact duplication of the most common *patola* textiles found in Indonesia, is a single piece of cloth decorated with an overall warp ikat design, a border along each edge, and *tumpal* at each end. The geometric designs filling the body of the cloth are nearly identical on most shawls. Other types of *adat* shawls portray people, boats, and animals. Lio shawls are generally worn only once each year for dancing during a special four-day *adat* festival, although on rare occasions they may be worn by the men as a shoulder or head cloth. Most families have these shawls and at least one is buried with every man.

The south coast town of Ende is known for ikat sarongs and shawls that resemble Lio weavings but are generally not as fine or as interesting. Previously, a few isolated inland villages produced large *adat* shawls worn only during ceremonies or on special occasions. The largest, finest pieces were apparently reserved for the village elders or leaders, called Musalaki. Today these shawls have virtually disappeared, for most were buried with their owners.

Beyond Lio, extending through most of eastern Flores, live the people of Sikka. There the women weave warp ikat sarongs composed of two wide mirror-image panels joined to form a five-foot high tube. Very tight weaving of thick handspun cotton thread produces a strong and heavy cloth. Virtually all women throughout the Sikka area spend most of every day weaving. Most pieces are kept folded in a cupboard and sold at market when the family needs money.

The overall design layout and coloration of sarongs are very similar throughout the Sikka kingdom. There are usually two wide horizontal bands—one toward the top and the other toward the bottom of the tube—that are identical to each other in design and color; series of narrower bands lie on either side of the wide bands. Sarongs are divided into color types by the use of red or blue as the background color of the two large bands. The ikat designs within the bands are usually white patterns on a dark ground but some pieces do have red and blue highlights. Although each village has its preferred designs and colors, there is no comprehensive design categorization as found in Lio.

In marked contrast to the small intricate designs of Lio, those on Sikka textiles are very bold, obviously reflecting strong *patola* and Dongson influences. Most typical are large circular motifs, snowflake-type designs, birds, and florals, with occasional stick-figure people. The women are free to create or copy whatever patterns they choose, and they have a great flair for incorporating any attractive motif into their design repertoire. It is common to see Lio motifs, Savu island designs, even Dutch cupids and swans.

There is also an older, more traditional type of ikat sarong which, as in Lio, probably predates the introduction of *patola*. It is a tube nearly seven feet long, composed of four joined sections decorated with a series of narrow blue and maroon brown bands containing simple white geometrics. Sometimes there are lizard and people motifs. Worn folded in half, they are found only on a few older women in the more remote villages.

Despite incursions of the modern world, Flores still remains remarkably unspoiled. True, the vast majority of textiles are now made with synthetic materials and lack the depth and beauty of the earlier weavings. But weavers are still prolific, and occasionally a new masterpiece is created using the traditional materials. After looking at both the old and the new there can be no doubt that Flores weavings form a rich and vital part of Indonesia's textile heritage.

Note
Thanks to John and Robyn Maxwell
for information on western Flores.

A village elder of central Flores wears the traditional Musalaki shawl, symbolic of his status and prestige in the village.

50
Sarong (skirt cloth)
Lio, Flores
Warp ikat
Cotton, rayon (?)
Warp: 190 cm.; weft: 133.3 cm.
Kent Watters
EX.77.196

This sarong belongs to one of the
oldest Lio design groups. The use
of ikat bands throughout the cloth
is typical of the older type and represents a style that existed prior to
the introduction of Indian *patola*
cloths. Constructed of four individual sections sewn along the
warp (horizontal in the illustration), this piece was originally
joined along the vertical edges and
formed a long tube when worn.
The dyed blue and white stripes
and the rows of white diamonds
give a rich textural feeling to the
somber dark ground.

51

Slendang (shoulder cloth)
Lio, Flores
Warp ikat
Cotton
Warp: 227.3 cm.; weft: 89 cm.
Los Angeles County Museum of Art
Costume Council and Museum
Associates Purchase
M.77.93.4
(See color plate, p. 20)

52

Man's Adat Shawl
Lio, Flores
Warp ikat
Cotton
Warp: 163.8 cm.; weft: 62.2 cm.
Los Angeles County Museum of Art
Costume Council and Museum
Associates Purchase
M.77.93.3

Worn on special occasions by a
Musalaki, or village elder, as a
symbol of position, this rare shawl
combines *patola* motifs and composition with the traditional central
Flores integration of multiple designs. The large lozenges appear to
float on a plane above the intricate
detailing that vibrates around them
and visually pulls them back into
the piece. Between the lozenges
pairs of little eyes stare powerfully
out at the world.

This *adat* shawl, worn once a year
during a dance ceremony, typifies
the deep, subtle colors and intricate
interlocking designs of Lio
ikat weaving.

53

Sarong (skirt cloth)
Lio, Flores
Warp ikat
Cotton
Warp: 142.2 cm.; weft: 177.9 cm.
Kent Watters
EX.77.246
(See color plate, p. 21)

This exceptional Lio sarong displays traditional design elements in the end panels and a remarkably unique composition in the center field, which was designed and executed directly from the weaver's vision with no preliminary drawing or models. Large chevrons formed by the intricate detailing of the center field are intersected by larger horizontal triangles that run the entire width of the field. Parallel vertical waves intensify the illusion of movement and of multiple planes. This subtle integration of several complex compositions de monstrates the highly developed technical and artistic sophistication of fine Lio ikat weaving.

54

Sarong (skirt cloth)
Manggarai area, western Flores
Brocade
Cotton
Warp: 152.7 cm.; weft: 114.3 cm.
Michael Yerby
EX.72.228

Ikat is the most common form of decoration on Flores textiles, but this sarong exhibits both a different technique and an unusual color sensibility. The blue ground is a balanced plain weave with brocading in four colors: pink, green, yellow, and white commercial spun threads. Small diamonds are brocaded in alternating bands except in the *kepala*, where the brocading is organized into tight bands of geometric designs. Although the designs in both halves match, the color sequence changes, which gives the piece a rather playful character. The symbolism, if any, of the motifs has not been identified.

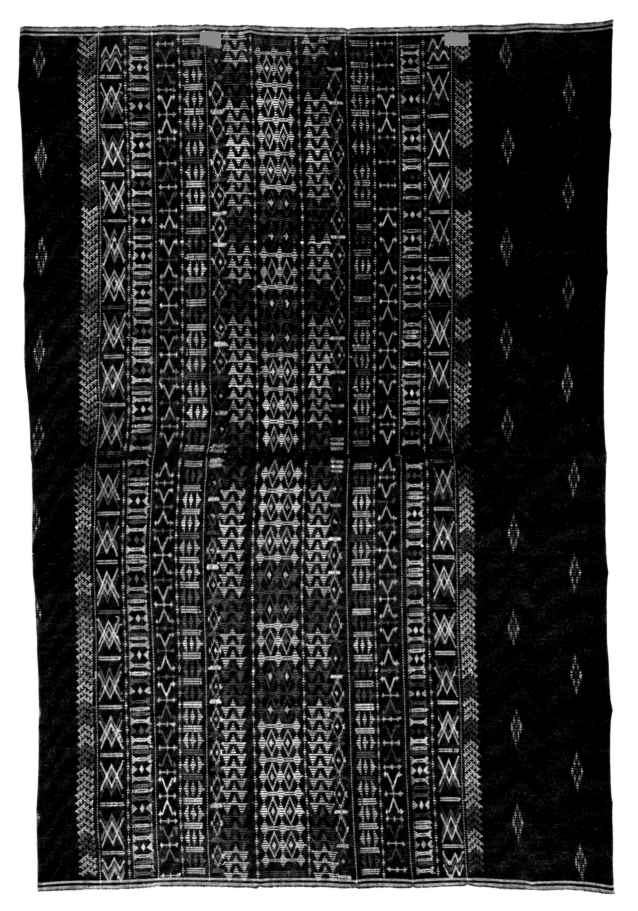

Kent Watters

Lomblen (known throughout Indonesia as Lembata), in the Solor Archipelago east of Flores, is a small, dry island dominated by several active volcanoes. Most of the rocky terrain consists of high, rolling hills covered with brush and gum trees. The inhabitants appear more Melanesian-Papuan than Malay, and animistic beliefs survive despite the widespread conversion to Catholicism. Weaving, a minor activity compared to food production and preparation, occurs mostly in the western half of the island, though it is also known in the eastern region of Kedang.

The western half of Lomblen is divided into two weaving areas corresponding to the north and south coasts. The people of Ille Api live on the north coast in numerous small villages scattered around the base of a large active volcano. Both the men and women wear heavy, handspun cotton sarongs constructed from two cloths sewn together. Usually woven in a series of solid bands of blue and brown, they are highlighted by brightly colored trade threads and occasionally by narrow bands of warp ikat designs toward the bottom of the tubes. The dyes are derived from the usual vegetable sources, primarily indigo leaves and the bark of *kombu* roots.

The most interesting textiles from Ille Api are the *adat* sarongs, which form part of a young woman's dowry and are worn only on special occasions. Composed of two mirror-image sections joined along the warp and sewn to form a tube, they are richly decorated with a series of bands alternating in width and containing various warp ikat designs, such as simple geometrics and eight-pointed stars. A pleasing use of red and blue highlights results in a clean, clear beauty that contrasts vividly with the dark, coarse cloths characteristic of most of these smaller islands.

Sarongs in the south coast area are similar to those in the north except that the woman's *adat* sarong tube consists of three joined sections and exhibits a wider range of decorative motifs. Two mirror-image end sections decorated with warp ikat bands flank a center section containing an overall ikat design. Sometimes these sarongs have as many as seven sections and may be nearly fifteen feet long. There are value classifications for these *adat* tubes directly related to the number of sections and the overall quality of workmanship. Unlike Flores, designs are not categorized and all women are allowed to weave.

Usually every young Lomblen woman, helped by her mother, will make two or three *adat* sarongs for her dowry. After that she will weave only everyday sarongs until her own daughter is preparing for marriage. The *adat* sarongs form an integral part of the marriage negotiations. The prospective husband must "buy" the daughter with a specified number of antique ivory tusks, and the prospective bride must reciprocate by presenting a dowry of ivory bracelets and *adat* sarongs. The husband becomes the owner of the sarongs and keeps them stored away; they are symbolic of the marriage union and are never worn or used. Occasionally they may be passed down to the couple's daughter to be added to her own few weavings, but most often they are buried with the husband.

There are two color types for *adat* sarongs; one has a dark maroon brown background with red and white ikat designs, the other a blue black background with patterns in white, red, and blue. Lightly dyed solid color threads are used for highlights, and often the juxtaposition of these threads creates a hybrid color. For example, pale indigo blue woven next to light yellow appears to be pastel green when viewed from a distance. This subtle color mixing is particularly effective in contrast to the somber background color of these *adat* sarongs. Unfortunately, brightly colored trade threads have now largely replaced the naturally dyed highlights.

The designs of Lomblen *adat* sarongs tend to be simpler than those in other areas of Indonesia, reflecting the original animistic beliefs of the people as well as a strong Dongson influence. The people firmly believe that any tampering with the traditional *adat* designs of one's family will bring sickness and death to the weaver or her relatives. Young women, therefore, weave only designs taught by their mothers; design sharing occurs only when a bride becomes a member of her husband's family. This is not to say that design innovation never occurs, however, for there are some examples of *patola*-influenced motifs such as elephants and medallions.

The most sacred and widely used design is the stylized figure of the manta ray. These mysterious marine creatures abound off the south coast of Lomblen, and as one sails in the small native outriggers, their large shadows can be seen gliding beneath the surface of the turquoise green water. It is not fully known why the manta ray is such a primary symbol, but it appears individually and in groups on nearly all *adat* sarongs (see no. 55). Other widely used motifs are the eight-pointed star, volcanic mountains, dancing stick-figure people, and bold geometrics, including *tumpal* borders.

Sometimes designs illustrate tribal legends. One rare piece depicts small figures climbing a volcano while others lie dead at the base beneath the ocean. Manta rays glide ominously over the bodies. It was explained that this chronicled the great wars that were fought to secure and hold tribal territory when the ancestors first migrated to the islands. The center piece of this sarong contains figures holding hands, symbolic of tribal unity.

Lomblen *adat* sarongs are coarse and the designs are simple, but it is this primitive quality combined with such ancient symbolic content that makes them unique and thus an important contribution to the traditional textiles of Indonesia.

55

Adat Sarong (ceremonial skirt cloth)
Lomblen
Warp ikat
Cotton
Warp: 111.7 cm.; weft: 203.2 cm.
Los Angeles County Museum of Art
Costume Council Fund
M.77.93.2
(See color plate, p. 22)

This traditional *adat* sarong was woven for a young woman's dowry, to be presented to the groom as part of the marriage exchange. Each family in Lomblen has its traditional designs, and design innovation or borrowing is strictly prohibited. The occasional example of *patola*-influenced designs, seen here in the center field, reveals some breakdown in the restrictions, but this is not common. The end panels of this piece show traditional mountain and stylized manta ray motifs.

James J. Fox

Nothing on the islands of Roti, Ndao, and Savu identifies persons more intimately than the houses in which they live and the cloth that they wear. Virtually all ceremonies of the life-cycle take place within the house, and cloth plays its part in all of them. Cloth swaddles the newly born, wraps and heals the sick, embraces and unites bride and groom, encloses the wedding bed and, in the end, enshrouds the dead.

This use of cloth in ceremonies within the houses of these islands is not a simple association but involves a profound relationship. On the island of Roti, for example, the building and roofing of houses by men is directly comparable to the dyeing and weaving of cloth by women. According to the myths, both activities have similar cultural origins and the one may not be begun while the other is in progress. Furthermore, on all of these islands, the word for house denotes not just a physical structure but also one's social group. Similarly, the designs and motifs that decorate traditional cloths are used to distinguish individuals according to their social group, class, and political domain. Yet each piece of cloth is a personal creation and no two pieces of traditional cloth are ever identical.

The three small islands of Roti, Ndao, and Savu lie between the large islands of Timor and Sumba. They are poor, dry, eroded, and densely populated, but they have long been centers of cultural vitality within the region. Historically, each island has developed its own separate culture in varied ways that are reflected in its tradition of textile design. Despite many differences, these traditions have enough in common to be discussed as a single group.

Cloth from these islands shares certain characteristics: 1) a highly developed use of ikat as the primary means of textile decoration; 2) a predominance of geometrical and botanical designs in three main colors— red, white, and blue black; 3) a general emphasis on finely tied, closely spaced motifs; and 4) the combination of many motifs into several distinctive design arrangements. The immediate impression that these cloths create is one of complex, concentrated formal ornamentation. They do not have the bold human or animal designs that make Sumbanese cloths so attractive, nor do they possess the elegant simplicity of cloth from Amarasi or Helong on Timor. On the contrary, cloth from these three islands exhibits some of the most complex and varied design arrangements within Indonesia.

Cloth from the three islands has approximately the same dimensions and much the same form. An important initial distinction is that between men's cloth and women's cloth. A man's cloth is rectangular with thread fringes at both ends. On Roti and Ndao, this is usually a single piece of woven cloth, whereas on Savu it consists of two similar but unequal pieces of cloth. Folded lengthwise along the line where these two pieces have been joined, the cloth will have an extra panel or band on one side. This is because all Savunese men's cloths are composed of bands and, although the number of these bands is not fixed, they must comprise an uneven number. In traditional dress, men wear two cloths: one wrapped around the waist, the other draped over the shoulder or worn across the chest. A woman's cloth, on the other hand, consists of an elongated sarong or tubular wrap worn folded in such a way that the middle section is never visible and, for this reason, has relatively little or no ikat decoration.

There is another important distinction crucial to understanding the textile traditions of these islands. On each island two kinds of cloth are generally recognized. First, there is truly traditional or ceremonial cloth whose every motif has social significance. This kind of cloth may only be worn by the appropriate person at the appropriate time. Such cloth is particularly important for mortuary ceremonies and, often, as individuals grow old they will put aside the cloth in which they wish to be buried. In contrast to ceremonial cloth is another kind that is more or less socially neutral. Such cloth is often beautifully executed, frequently interesting for its artistic innovation, and much more commonly worn than ceremonial cloth. Both kinds of cloth are part of each island's tradition and must be considered and compared with one another.

Unless one is able to recognize traditional motifs, it is often difficult to distinguish ordinary cloth from ceremonial cloth. To complicate matters, ordinary cloth may be composed of traditional motifs combined with non-traditional motifs such as birds, roses, little angels, or patterns copied from the cloths of other islands. The effect of this mixing of motifs is to neutralize the social or ceremonial significance of the cloth but this, too, is not without meaning, for such cloth invariably indicates something about its owner.

As these cultures have undergone change, the distinction between ordinary cloth and ceremonial cloth has continued on Savu, has been more flexibly interpreted on Roti but, within this present generation, has ceased to be observed on Ndao. In addition, new forms of cloth have developed on the three islands. The most popular is a reduced version of a man's cloth which is generally called a "scarf." Despite its appearance, this cloth is not worn by men but only by women or children. Young girls who are learning to ikat usually begin by making these scarfs, and since they are not ceremonial pieces, they show a great deal of artistic experimentation. On Savu a minor industry has recently been organized to produce large numbers of these small pieces in a more or less standard format for sale to tourists. In this regard, one final remark is worth making. For cultural reasons Savunese women's cloth and Rotinese men's cloth are objects of more social attention and elaboration than their counterparts. This has been especially evident in recent years as Savunese women and Rotinese men have sought to retain their traditional dress.

Roti, Ndao, and Savu each has its own separate language. From a purely linguistic point of view, the languages of Roti and Savu stand far apart from one another and seem to represent the migrations of separate groups of Austronesians into the area many centuries ago. With such different languages, it is surprising that these two islands share as many cultural similarities as they do. A key to understanding some of this cultural sharing is to be found on the island of Ndao, which lies less than a mile off the western tip of Roti. Both literally and figuratively, the Ndaonese have been the middlemen between the two cultures, and in the process their own culture has been radically transformed.

The Ndaonese are clearly an offshoot of the Savunese people. Their language and ancient traditions make this abundantly evident. Yet for many centuries they have developed these traditions in close proximity to the Rotinese. Their island is so small, so poor, and so dry that it does not have the resources to support its population; hence many Ndaonese have settled on Roti and have gradually been assimilated. Those who have chosen to stay on Ndao have developed a specialization that has enabled them to continue to inhabit their island. Virtually every man on Ndao is a gold- or silversmith. Every dry season the men leave their island to work gold and silver into jewelry in return for food or animals that they bring back to Ndao before the rainy season begins. In their absence, the women of Ndao weave.

Originally, Ndaonese cloth was like that of Savu, and it undoubtedly had a major influence on the development of Rotinese cloth. According to Rotinese myths, the art of weaving came from the island of Ndao, as did some of the most important ceremonial motifs. In turn, the design of Ndaonese cloth was affected by the same historical influences that affected other textile traditions of the region, particularly those of Roti.

The people of Roti, Ndao, and Savu were among the first in the archipelago to come into regular contact with Europeans. In the early part of the seventeenth century the Portuguese visited the islands and made brief attempts to establish missions. By the middle of the century, however, various local rulers had allied themselves with the Dutch and agreed to trade exclusively with the Dutch East India Company.

The Dutch recognized four or five local rulers on Savu and they began by offering formal recognition to about the same number on Roti. But on Roti this turned into a scramble for official recognition. The number of recognized rulers on the island quickly rose from six to twelve and, by the end of the eighteenth century, the number of rulers had gone from twelve to eighteen, with still another ruler for Ndao. At stake were a number of trade prerogatives.

Trade was conducted at an elite level. Each ruler or "regent" would provide a tribute—in slaves, wax, and foodstuffs—from his domain in return for muskets, gin, and royal regalia, which consisted mainly of silk *patola* cloth. In the documents of the period, this cloth was often referred to as "patola zouratta" since it came from an area of Gujarat in the vicinity of the town of Surat.

The Dutch awarded *patola* cloth only to the highest rulers with whom they traded, and the right to wear this cloth became the exclusive prerogative of the top nobility on each island. When the Company went bankrupt and *patola* cloth became scarce, the nobility adopted *patola* motifs for their own ikat cloth. This process went furthest on Roti. Certain noblemen's cloths are near replicas, on a reduced scale, of silk *patola* (see no. 57). The women of all three islands also adopted various *patola* motifs as status markers. The most important of these motifs is a kind of eight-pointed flower centered within a circle that even today may only be worn by a person of noble descent. Savunese men, on the other hand, adopted no *patola* motifs in their cloth.

The fact that we can document *patola* influence is a great aid in understanding the development of these textile traditions. But equally important is the social environment within which these cloths are used. Since this differs from island to island, we must consider each island separately.

The Savunese, as might be judged from their textiles, are tenaciously proud of their traditions. Social organization on the island is complex and some areas still preserve intact the entire cycle of their old religious ceremonies. Savu, including the offshore island of Rai Jua, is divided into various domains or ceremonial territories, each with its own priesthood. These domains are, in turn, divided into villages, which mainly comprise the residence of one clan or lineage. Savu is thus made up of numerous exclusive and generally squabbling residential groups. As a rule, an individual belongs to the residence group or clan of his father. What unites the island is a kind of dual organization or moiety system. Not only does an individual belong to the clan of his father, he also belongs to one of two groups according to his mother. These all-important groups are called "Blossoms" in Savunese, and they are distinguished from one another as the "Greater Blossom" *(Hubi Ae)* and the "Lesser Blossom" *(Hubi Iki)*. Each Blossom is divided into approximately six named subgroups, which are referred to as *Wini* or "Seeds."

Savu seems to present a curious paradox. For three centuries Savunese men have been renowned as the most daring warriors in the region. Furthermore, the priesthood that organizes the public ceremonies in each territory is wholly masculine. Yet in certain important realms the island is dominated by women, since an essential portion of social knowledge is their exclusive preserve. Men will know which Blossom they belong to, but they will rarely know more than that. Women know about the Seeds, and this knowledge is crucial for the arrangement of marriages as well as for many aspects of life-cycle ceremonies, particularly funerals. But knowledge about these groups is not open to discussion; in fact, it is not transmitted verbally. Rather, it is passed on from mother to daughter as a visual display system embodied in the motifs on women's sarongs. Thus each large motif on women's ceremonial sarongs signifies a particular Seed within one of the two female Blossoms (see no. 60). These motifs are so important that, it is said, if ever a woman dared to wear the wrong sarong at a funeral, other women would tear it from her body and drive her away.

To begin to understand the social significance of Savunese cloth, one needs at least a half-dozen pieces. For our purposes here, it will be sufficient to distinguish the cloth of one Blossom from the other. One clue to this distinction involves the dyeing of the cloth. The cloth of the Greater Blossom is dyed in a deeper, darker indigo blue and in a brighter, clearer red. In contrast, the cloth of the Lesser Blossom is dyed in a lighter blue, and if red is used at all, it is generally muted.

The island of Roti presents a number of contrasts with Savu. The Rotinese pride themselves on their openness to new ideas, on the heterogeneity of their culture, and on the many differences that distinguish one group of Rotinese from another. In the early eighteenth century several Rotinese rulers became Christians, developed their own schools, and made the island an area of cultural innovation. All Rotinese still identify themselves in terms of the eighteen domains recognized by the Dutch East India Company, and there is enough dialect variation on the island to allow the Rotinese to claim that each of the eighteen domains has its own "language." Moreover, Rotinese culture seems to have developed on a principle of addition. New influences have been accepted without rejection of the old. Ancient ceremonial rules combine with political and religious traditions of the colonial period in a curious amalgam of customary ways. The Rotinese insist that nothing should be simple, and this is certainly true of their textile traditions.

Cloth, particularly men's cloth, may carry so much meaning and embody so many disparate influences that it is difficult to begin a discussion of it. Some cloth is made to conform to ancient patterns, others show innovations that have occurred in the last two or three hundred years.

One way of approaching this variety in men's cloth is to distinguish between those pieces that are composed exclusively of bands and those that possess center fields. It is probable that all men's cloth was once composed of bands like men's cloth from Savu, Ndao, or Timor. However, unlike Savunese cloth, which must have an uneven number of bands, Rotinese cloth must have an even number of such bands. Savunese cloth is thus structured on a principle of asymmetry, whereas Rotinese cloth is intentionally symmetrical. In this regard, Rotinese men's cloth is comparable to cloth from areas on neighboring Timor, such as Helong,

Amarasi, or Molo. But there is one signal difference. Cloth from these three Timorese areas has a wide, undyed white center band, whereas the oldest type of Rotinese cloth has a broad, black-dyed center band.

According to the myths, many of the motifs on Rotinese cloth originated from the dismemberment of a creature (or creatures) identified with the shark and crocodile. The blood, flesh, and inner organs of this creature were divided among the domains, giving them their distinctive motifs. The killing of the shark and crocodile is supposed to have occurred on or near Ndao and, not surprisingly, one of the most reptilianlike motifs is said to derive from Ndao. In Rotinese this is simply called the "red motif," and although it is sometimes described as the skin of the crocodile, it resembles the dappled skin of a python. This is one of the most common motifs on banded cloths. Another important traditional band motif consists of a succession of what are referred to as "flowers," though their appearance is more that of tiny leaves or flowerbuds on intertwining stems or on stems that emerge from a central lozenge. A modern version of this motif, which is also found on some Savunese cloth, is composed of a string of roses.

The social significance of banded cloth with ceremonial motifs lies in the fact that its pattern predates the status distinctions introduced by *patola* motifs. Hence this cloth can be worn by nobles and commoners alike. But *patola* motifs did more than introduce status emblems. The introduction of these motifs changed the whole design arrangement of men's cloth from bands to broad center fields. The use of center fields, in turn, opened up a whole new range of design possibilities, many of which are completely free of *patola* motifs. One good example of this is the use of the "red motif." On banded cloth this motif appears as a number of separate undulating pythons, while on cloth with a center field this same motif may be recreated as a complex group of interlocking snakes or, alternatively, it may be reproduced geometrically to appear as a lattice. The possibilities are innumerable.

In general, however, cloth with center fields shows its *patola* origins. At both ends of the cloth are lateral bands of *tumpal* motifs which are common to many Indonesian textiles and, in Roti, are almost certainly derived from *patola* cloth. In Rotinese these two lateral end bands are referred to as "heads" and each is flanked by another set of lateral bands composed of flowerlike lozenges or diamonds. This second band divides the "head" from the center field, or "body," of the cloth.

Since the lateral bands are much the same on all cloth, they carry no special social meaning. Only the center fields contain motifs that identify their owner, though how these are arranged is left to the woman who designs the cloth. A center field may consist of several "blocks" of motifs with borders on either side (see no. 57), or it may contain a single continuous pattern extending across the width of the cloth.

There are three specific motifs that identify a cloth as a noble's cloth. One of these is the eight-pointed *patola* flower also found on noble women's sarongs throughout the region. The other two motifs are more specifically associated with central Roti, the seat of one of the oldest and most powerful domains on the islands. In this area a cloth containing any or all of these three motifs contrasts with a cloth that has a generalized geometrical "flower" pattern (see no. 56). This pattern may be produced in many ways, but it usually gives the appearance of a vine-tangle with blossoms and leaves. In central Roti this is decidedly a "commoner" pattern but this distinction cannot be generalized for the entire island. In west Roti, for example, where this is a particularly popular pattern, it has less lowly connotations, while in east Roti where this pattern also occurs, it contrasts with a variety of motifs that seem to come from ceremonial designs on banded cloth. Thus the provenance of a cloth, which is often suggested by the style in which it is tied, will provide some idea of the significance of its motifs. The patterns on cloth from east and central Roti tend to be more tightly tied, giving them a smaller or finer look than similar patterns on cloth from west Roti. Add to this the possibility of mixing motifs—both traditional and modern—and one begins to have some appreciation of the subtleties involved in interpreting this cloth.

Ndaonese cloth reflects the traditions of both Savu and Roti. A generation ago some Ndaonese women's cloth was virtually indistinguishable from Savunese cloth, while other pieces closely resembled women's cloth from Roti. The same was not quite true for men's cloth, which had changed much earlier to conform to Rotinese standards, although some cloth continued to be based on the asymmetry of an uneven number of bands.

Specific reasons for this are not hard to discover. For centuries the men of Ndao have left their island in the dry season to ply their special craft of jewelry making. The majority went to Roti, and it became a common practice for Ndaonese men to take orders for Rotinese-type cloth to be produced on Ndao. They would take back with them to Ndao samples of the old cloth that their wives and daughters were supposed to copy. Eventually the cloth that Ndaonese women produced for Roti influenced the cloth that they produced for themselves. In time this piecework became a major home industry.

Today every woman on Ndao is involved in tying, dyeing, and weaving cloth. Almost all of this cloth is made for sale to Rotinese, whose women are rapidly abandoning the arts of tying and weaving. The effect of this on Ndao has been considerable, and the work now provides a sizeable income for the island. To meet the demand, cloth is produced in large quantities with purchased thread and chemical dyes. Formerly each cloth was tied separately; now several cloths may be tied at once. The introduc-

tion of new colors—yellow, green, orange—has greatly increased the complexity of the ikat process, while the simultaneous tying of a number of pieces has forced an enlargement of all motifs. The result is a lively cloth with bright, striking patterns but by comparison with traditional pieces, this cloth may appear almost garish.

An even greater change has occurred in the use of motifs. Motifs have a purely decorative, not a social function. Although some cloth is a direct copy of Rotinese cloth, other cloth consists of a total jumble of motifs. Motifs from Savunese or Ndaonese women's cloth have been reproduced, for example, on the center fields of what purport to be Rotinese men's cloth.

Only in the last five years has tourist demand for ikat cloth begun to have impact on the three islands. This demand has been greatest for Savunese cloth. Ndaonese cloth is still primarily bought and worn by Rotinese. The mass production and commercialization of cloth that has now begun will undoubtedly produce profound changes in the textile tradition of the three islands.

56

Pou Dula Bunga (woman's skirt cloth)
Roti
Warp ikat
Cotton
Warp: 141 cm.; weft: 114.3 cm.
Los Angeles County Museum of Art
Costume Council Fund
M.77.81.28

The simple flower pattern on this commoner's cloth provides a characteristic, if modest, example of the design arrangement on Rotinese women's cloths.

Lafa Dula Penis no Dula Nggeo
(man's cloth)
Termanu, Roti
Warp ikat
Cotton
Warp: 182.9 cm.; weft: 69.2 cm.
Los Angeles County Museum of Art
Costume Council and Museum
Associates Purchase
M.77.112

The influence of *patola* cloth is clearly seen in the lateral bands at both ends and in the two blocks of motifs in the center field, which identify this cloth as a noble one. Each block contains six separate motifs, arranged in pairs. The middle two are clearly recognizable *patola* motifs known on Roti as *dula nggeo* or the "black motif." Flanking these are two pairs of a similar motif called *dula penis*.

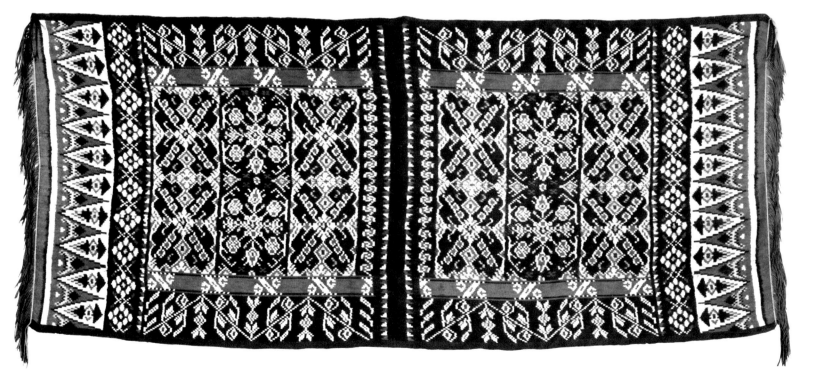

58

Selimut (man's cloth)
Seba, Savu
Warp ikat
Cotton
Warp: 172.7 cm.; weft: 90.1 cm.
Los Angeles County Museum of Art
Costume Council Fund
M.73.73.9

59

Selimut (man's cloth)
Savu
Warp ikat
Cotton
Warp: 104.1 cm.; weft: 76.8 cm.
Kent Watters
EX.77.205
(See color plate, p. 23)

This ceremonial man's cloth of the Greater Blossom group consists of nine bands with various narrow interbands. Each band is decorated with two alternating motifs, one known as *moto* ("star"), the other as *boda*. This cloth shows the basic form of both motifs.

This is a beautifully designed Savunese man's cloth with subtly arranged interbands. Since the motifs are not ceremonial, this cloth could be worn by a member of either Blossom. The use of red in the center of each motif suggests, however, that this cloth was made for use by someone from the Greater Blossom.

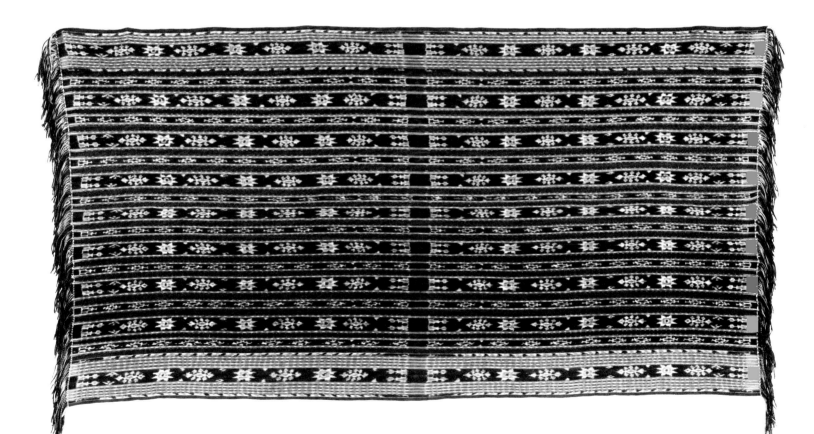

60
Sarong (skirt cloth)
Savu
Warp ikat
Cotton
Warp: 208.3 cm.; weft: 75.6 cm.
Los Angeles County Museum of Art
Costume Council Fund
M.73.73.29

Each of the bands on a Savunese
woman's cloth is named. The combination of the motifs in the bands
and, in particular, the main motif
called *hebe* identify the owner according to the Blossom and the
Seed groups to which she belongs.
This cloth belonged to a woman
from the Greater Blossom.

Mary Hunt Kahlenberg

Timor is the largest of the Lesser Sunda Islands (300 miles long and 60 miles wide). For several hundred years it was divided between two European countries: the western portion was a Dutch colony; the eastern portion remained a Portuguese territory until fairly recently. Kupang, the largest town on the island, has a mixed population of peoples from the other Lesser Sunda Islands, particularly Savu and Roti, as well as Indo-Europeans and Chinese. As these immigrants have settled on the coast and in the larger villages, the indigenous Timor people have gradually retreated to the mountains and more inaccessible regions.

As yet, there has not been a thorough study of Timor textiles. Although some resemble textiles woven on the other islands, Timor fabrics have certain apparently unique characteristics, particularly the use of single image designs; a wide range of techniques, including ikat, supplementary weft, tapestry, and card-weaving; and many bright colors, especially combinations of red, orange, and pink. Although the dyes used to produce these colors are synthetic and therefore not traditional, the juxtaposition of colors appears to reflect a traditional color sense.

Selimut, worn by both men and women as either a shoulder wrap or skirt, are constructed in three vertical sections. The individual widths of the pieces are narrow by comparison to those woven in the other islands, but when sewn together they produce a wider textile. These *selimut* are wrapped around the waist, folded across the front, and then rolled at the top. An additional sash or cloth is sometimes worn around the waist and folded or tied in front.

Two basic variations of the *selimut* occur: one has a central ikat panel and warp-striped borders, the other has a supplementary weft center with warp-striped and ikat borders. Although there are distinctive designs from each region, these two basic formats appear to be ubiquitous. Textiles with central ikat panels frequently show stylized anthropomorphs and birds, as in no. 62, where spotted figures span the entire width of the ikat panel. The commanding frontal stance with raised arms and upturned palms is a symbol of the protection that the cloth transfers to the wearer. Textiles using the supplementary weft technique generally feature smaller, sparser designs such as the small birds in no. 61. The small scale and fine detail of this technique contrast with the wide white bands and colorful stripes of the rest of the textile to produce a richness of texture and color.

Many textiles are made in the Lesser Sunda Islands for trade to other islands that do not have a textile tradition, particularly Irian Barat. Most of these are distinctly different from textiles worn and used on Timor. Generally referred to as *kain Timor,* they feature stripes and simple ikat patterns. It is possible that some are actually woven solely for export, either by the Timorese or some of the immigrant peoples. It is equally

possible that they are woven on one of the other textile-producing islands and just pass through the ports of Timor, which are a major stopping point for ships sailing to the more eastern islands.

A man photographed near Insoma, Timor, wears a warp-striped and ikat kain, *encircled around the middle by a row of birds.*

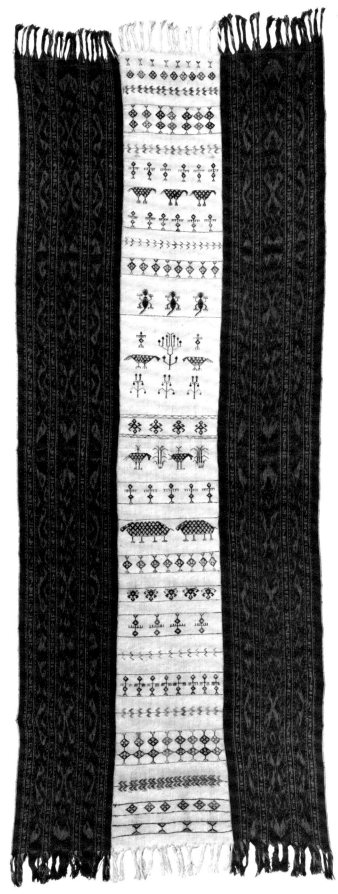

Selimut (man's cloth)
Timor
Warp ikat, supplementary warp,
supplementary weft
Cotton
Warp: 190.5 cm.; weft: 78.8 cm.
Jeff Holmgren and Anita Spertus
EX.77.253

A three-section cloth is traditional
in Timor. In the center section,
supplementary weft yarns draw delightful abstracted animals and anthropomorphs. These are flanked by
ikat panels of rhombs bordered
with narrow stripes of small
geometric supplementary warp
designs.

62
Selimut (man's cloth), detail
Miomfo, Timor
Warp ikat
Cotton
Warp: 205.8 cm.; weft: 114.3 cm.
Kent Watters
EX.77.206

The large spotted anthropomorphic figures of this cloth are a traditional and dynamic aspect of the Timor *selimut*. These figures develop one out of the other, suggesting the concept of spiritual protection known throughout Indonesia. The flexed limbs, upturned hands, and ear "keys" are elements that suggest motifs from Sarawak, Sumba, and South Sumatra.

Kisar

Sarong (skirt cloth)
Kampung Wonreli, Kisar
Warp ikat
Cotton
Warp: 137.2 cm.; weft: 76.2 cm.
Textile Museum
EX.77.279

The combination of dark blue and brown handspun yarns with a large amount of commercially spun and dyed red and narrow stripes of natural yellow and green distinguishes this sarong from those of the neighboring Savu and Roti islands. The childlike quality of the ikat animals and orant figures is particularly delightful. Most Indonesian ikat sarongs are made from several lengths of ikat and stripe panels sewn together horizontally, which means that the warp ikat pattern encircles the body, rather than running vertically as on the loom.

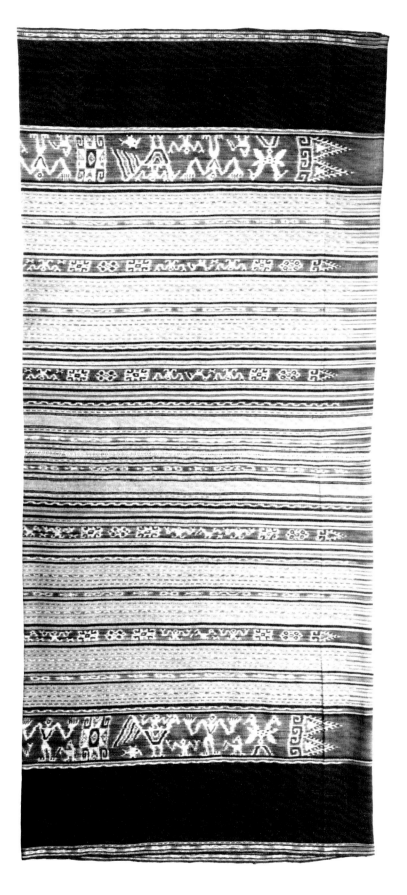

Sumbawa

Sarong (skirt cloth)
Sumbawa
Supplementary weft on plain weave
Cotton, metallic foil
Warp: 120.7 cm.; weft: 81.9 cm.
Los Angeles County Museum of Art
Costume Council Fund
M.75.79
(See color plate, p. 24)

This lavish ceremonial sarong displays a special sophistication in the
layering of metallic *songket* (supplementary weft) over a ground of
small red and black plaid. Of
modified *patola* origins, the large
field pattern has flowers within a
geometric enclosure and a top and
bottom floral border (see *patola*
illustration in glossary).   MHK

Sumatra

Sarong (skirt cloth)
Sumatra
Supplementary weft
Silk, metallic threads
Warp: 210.9 cm.; weft: 78.8 cm.
Gift of Mrs. Helen Cannon Rowen
65.24

Tapis (skirt cloth)
Lampong, South Sumatra
Embroidery
Cotton, sequins, mica
Warp: 109.2 cm.; weft: 111.8 cm.
Costume Council Fund
M.69.60

Sarong (skirt cloth)
Sumatra
Supplementary weft
Silk, metallic threads
Warp: 152.4 cm.; weft: 123.1 cm.
Gift of Mrs. Dorothy M. Crane
69.33.3

Sarong (skirt cloth)
Abung, East Sumatra
Embroidery, supplementary weft
Cotton
Warp: 124.4 cm.; weft: 132.6 cm.
Costume Council Fund
M.73.26.1

Tapis (skirt cloth)
Lampong, South Sumatra
Embroidery
Cotton, mica
Warp: 134.7 cm.; weft: 214.4 cm.
Costume Council Fund
M.73.26.2

Sarong (man's skirt cloth)
South Sumatra
Supplementary weft
Silk, metallic threads
Warp: 179.1 cm.; weft: 224.8 cm.
Gift of Mrs. A. S. Loebis
M.73.69.1

Slendang (shoulder cloth)
South Sumatra
Supplementary weft
Silk, metallic threads
Warp: 200 cm.; weft: 121.3 cm.
Gift of Mrs. A. S. Loebis
M.73.69.2

Tapis (skirt cloth)
South Sumatra
Embroidery, appliqué, supplementary
weft
Cotton, wool, mica, metallic threads
Warp: 122.5 cm.; weft: 121.3 cm.
Gift of Mrs. Rudolph Liebig
M.73.70

Tapis (skirt cloth)
Lampong, South Sumatra
Weft ikat, embroidery, supplementary
weft
Cotton, silk, mica
Warp: 125.2 cm.; weft: 122.6 cm.
Costume Council Fund
M.73.73.1

Tapis (skirt cloth)
South Sumatra
Embroidery
Cotton, mica
Warp: 132 cm.; weft: 109.8 cm.
Costume Council Fund
M.73.73.2

Tapis (skirt cloth)
Lampong, South Sumatra
Appliqué, supplementary weft
Cotton, wool, sequins, metallic threads
Warp: 127 cm.; weft: 126.4 cm.
Costume Council Fund
M.73.73.3

Palepai (ceremonial cloth)
South Sumatra
Supplementary weft
Cotton
Warp: 337 cm.; weft: 62.2 cm.
Costume Council Fund
M.73.73.6

Kain Kepala (head cloth)
South Sumatra
Weft ikat, supplementary weft
Silk, metallic threads
Warp: 81.3 cm.; weft: 81.9 cm.
Costume Council Fund
M.73.73.13

Jacket
South Sumatra
Embroidery
Cotton, mica, sequins, shells
Length: 55.8 cm.; bottom width:
108 cm.
Costume Council Fund
M.73.73.14

Tampan (ceremonial cloth)
South Sumatra
Supplementary weft
Cotton
Warp: 68.6 cm.; weft: 61 cm.
Costume Council Fund
M.73.73.28

Sarong (skirt cloth)
Sumatra
Plain weave
Silk
Warp: 111.8 cm.; weft: 118 cm.
Gift of Mrs. A. S. Loebis
CR.74.26.1

Kain Kepala (head cloth)
South Sumatra
Batik
Cotton
Warp: 92.1 cm.; weft: 90.2 cm.
Costume Council Fund
M.74.18.1

Tapis (skirt cloth)
Sumatra
Weft ikat, brocade
Silk, metallic threads
Warp: 227.3 cm.; weft: 123.2 cm.
Costume Council Fund
M.74.18.7

Tampan (ceremonial cloth)
South Sumatra
Supplementary weft
Cotton, silk
Warp: 50.8 cm.; weft: 66 cm.
Costume Council Fund
M.77.81.1

Tampan (ceremonial cloth)
South Sumatra
Supplementary weft
Cotton, silk, metallic threads
Warp: 63.5 cm.; weft: 70 cm.
Costume Council Fund
M.77.81.2

Tampan (ceremonial cloth)
South Sumatra
Supplementary weft
Cotton, silk
Warp: 71.8 cm.; weft: 66 cm.
Costume Council Fund
M.77.81.3

Tampan (ceremonial cloth)
South Sumatra
Supplementary weft
Cotton
Warp: 61 cm.; weft: 54.7 cm.
Costume Council Fund
M.77.81.5

Tampan (ceremonial cloth)
South Sumatra
Supplementary weft
Cotton, silk, metallic strips
Warp: 55.2 cm.; weft: 52.3 cm.
Costume Council Fund
M.77.81.6

Tampan (ceremonial cloth)
South Sumatra
Supplementary weft
Cotton, silk
Warp: 54.3 cm.; weft: 48.8 cm.
Costume Council Fund
M.77.81.7

Tampan (ceremonial cloth)
South Sumatra
Supplementary weft
Cotton, silk, metallic threads
Warp: 51.1 cm.; weft: 46.3 cm.
Costume Council Fund
M.77.81.8

Tampan (ceremonial cloth)
South Sumatra
Supplementary weft
Cotton, silk, metallic threads
Warp: 55 cm.; weft: 52 cm.
Costume Council Fund
M.77.81.9

Tampan (ceremonial cloth)
South Sumatra
Supplementary weft
Cotton
Warp: 50.1 cm.; weft: 43.9 cm.
Costume Council Fund
M.77.81.10

Tampan (ceremonial cloth)
South Sumatra
Supplementary weft
Cotton
Warp: 45.8 cm.; weft: 47 cm.
Costume Council Fund
M.77.81.11

Tampan (ceremonial cloth)
South Sumatra
Supplementary weft
Cotton, silk
Warp: 47.7 cm.; weft: 48.2 cm.
Costume Council Fund
M.77.81.12

Tampan (ceremonial cloth)
South Sumatra
Supplementary weft
Cotton, silk
Warp: 36.1 cm.; weft: 41.2 cm.
Costume Council Fund
M.77.81.13

Tampan (ceremonial cloth)
South Sumatra
Supplementary weft
Cotton, silk, metallic strips and threads
Warp: 38.8 cm.; weft: 45.8 cm.
Costume Council Fund
M.77.81.16

Tatibin (ceremonial cloth)
South Sumatra
Supplementary weft
Cotton, metallic threads
Warp: 101 cm.; weft: 43.1 cm.
Costume Council Fund
M.77.81.18

Tatibin (ceremonial cloth)
South Sumatra
Supplementary weft
Cotton, silk, metallic threads
Warp: 120.3 cm.; weft: 38.1 cm.
Costume Council Fund
M.77.81.20

Palepai (ceremonial cloth)
South Sumatra
Supplementary weft
Cotton, silk, metallic strips
Warp: 142.9 cm.; weft: 273.7 cm.
Costume Council Fund
M.77.81.21

Tampan (ceremonial cloth)
South Sumatra
Supplementary weft
Cotton, silk
Warp: 57.8 cm.; weft: 51.5 cm.
Costume Council Fund
M.77.81.22

Tampan (ceremonial cloth)
South Sumatra
Supplementary weft
Cotton
Warp: 71.1 cm.; weft: 65.4 cm.
Costume Council Fund
M.77.81.23

Tampan (ceremonial cloth)
South Sumatra
Supplementary weft
Cotton, metallic strips and threads
Warp: 94 cm.; weft: 43.1 cm.
Costume Council Fund
M.77.81.24

Kain Prada (gold cloth)
Palembang, Sumatra
Batik
Cotton, gold leaf
Warp: 119.8 cm.; weft: 82 cm.
Costume Council and Museum
Associates Purchase
M.77.92

Sarong (skirt cloth)
Menangkabau, West Sumatra
Supplementary weft
Silk, metallic threads
Warp: 80.3 cm.; weft: 143.5 cm.
Costume Council and Museum
Associates Purchase
TR.2156

Tampan (ceremonial cloth)
South Sumatra
Supplementary weft
Cotton, silk
Warp: 83.8 cm.; weft: 70 cm.
Costume Council and Museum
Associates Purchase
TR.2159.1

Tampan (ceremonial cloth)
South Sumatra
Supplementary weft
Cotton
Warp: 66 cm.; weft: 62.2 cm.
Costume Council and Museum
Associates Purchase
TR.2159.2

Tampan (ceremonial cloth)
South Sumatra
Supplementary weft
Cotton
Warp: 65.5 cm.; weft: 62.8 cm.

Costume Council and Museum
Associates Purchase
TR.2159.3

Sarong (skirt cloth)
South Sumatra
Batik
Cotton
Warp: 191.1 cm.; weft: 86.3 cm.
Costume Council and Museum
Associates Purchase
TR.2186.2

Borneo

Bidang (woman's skirt cloth)
Mahakam, Indonesian Borneo (Bahau)
Warp ikat
Cotton
Warp: 96.5 cm.; weft: 78.8 cm.
Costume Council Fund
M.77.81.25

Kalambi (man's jacket)
Mahakam River area, Indonesian Borneo
(Kenyah)
Plain weave, appliqué
Cotton, bast fiber, trade beads, brass
bells
Length: 33 cm.; bottom width:
128.2 cm.
Costume Council Fund
M.77.81.27

Pua (ceremonial cloth)
Batang Lupar River, Sarawak,
Malaysian Borneo (Iban)
Warp ikat
Cotton
Warp: 179.2 cm.; weft: 88.9 cm.
Costume Council and Museum
Associates Purchase
M.77.113.2

Pua (ceremonial cloth)
Batang Lupar River, Sarawak,
Malaysian Borneo (Iban)
Warp ikat
Cotton

Warp: 182.9 cm.; weft: 91.4 cm.
Costume Council and Museum
Associates Purchase
M.77.113.3

Bidang (woman's skirt cloth)
Kapit, Sarawak, Malaysian Borneo
(Iban)
Warp ikat
Cotton
Warp: 110.5 cm.; weft: 58.4 cm.
Costume Council and Museum
Associates Purchase
TR.2188.5

Bidang (woman's skirt cloth)
Upper Balch River, Sarawak, Malaysian
Bornco (Iban)
Warp ikat
Cotton
Warp: 115.6 cm.; weft: 53.3 cm.
Costume Council and Museum
Associates Purchase
TR.2188.6

Bidang (woman's skirt cloth)
Sibu, Sarawak, Malaysian Borneo (Iban)
Warp ikat
Cotton
Warp: 114.9 cm.; weft: 44.5 cm.
Costume Council and Museum
Associates Purchase
TR.2188.7

Celebes

Ceremonial Cloth
Galumpang, Celebes (Toraja)
Warp ikat
Cotton
Warp: 163.3 cm.; weft: 153.8 cm.
Costume Council Fund
M.74.14

Sekomandi or Lelesepun (funeral shroud)
Rongkong, Celebes (Toraja)
Warp ikat
Cotton

Warp: 264.1 cm.; weft: 170.1 cm.
Costume Council Fund
M.77.20.2

Java

Kain Kepala (head cloth)
Central Java
Batik
Cotton
Warp: 100.7 cm.; weft: 103.6 cm.
Gift of Miss Jessie M. Tilney
42.29.2

Kain Kepala (head cloth)
Java
Batik
Cotton
Warp: 94 cm.; weft: 98.2 cm.
Gift of Miss Jessie M. Tilney
42.29.3

Slendang (shoulder cloth)
Java
Batik
Cotton
Warp: 63.5 cm.; weft: 104.2 cm.
Gift of Miss Jessie M. Tilney
42.29.5

Kain Kepala (head cloth)
Java
Batik
Cotton
Warp: 105.5 cm.; weft: 105.5 cm.
Gift of Miss Jessie M. Tilney
42.29.6

Kain Kepala (head cloth)
Java
Batik
Cotton
Warp: 69.5 cm.; weft: 106 cm.
Gift of Miss Jessie M. Tilney
42.29.7

Pillow Cover
Java
Batik

Cotton
Warp: 97.2 cm.; weft: 53.4 cm.
Gift of Miss Jessie M. Tilney
42.29.9

Kain Kepala (head cloth)
Java
Batik
Cotton
Warp: 104 cm.; weft: 105.5 cm.
Gift of Mrs. Preston H. Mc Clelland
CR.91.57.1a

Kain Panjang (skirt cloth)
North coast, Java
Batik
Cotton
Warp: 234.3 cm.; weft: 105.4 cm.
Gift of Mr. Norman M. Kelly
CR.233.62.2

Sarong (skirt cloth)
Java
Batik
Cotton
Warp: 197 cm.; weft: 103.5 cm.
Gift of Mr. Norman M. Kelly
CR.233.62.3

Kain Panjang (skirt cloth)
Java
Batik
Cotton
Warp: 243.8 cm.; weft: 106.7 cm.
Gift of Mrs. James Porter Fiske
CR.14.64.10

Slendang (shoulder cloth)
North coast, Java
Batik
Cotton
Warp: 304.8 cm.; weft: 59.7 cm.
Gift of Harold W. Grieve
CR.82.65.3

Sarong (skirt cloth)
North coast, Java
Batik
Cotton

Warp: 191.8 cm.; weft: 105.4 cm.
Gift of Harold W. Grieve
CR.82.65.4

Sarong (skirt cloth)
Cirebon, north coast, Java
Batik
Cotton
Warp: 196.8 cm.; weft: 105.4 cm.
Costume Council Fund
M.73.73.12

Kain Panjang (skirt cloth)
North coast, Java
Batik
Cotton
Warp: 246.4 cm.; weft: 102.9 cm.
Costume Council Fund
M.73.73.15

Kain Panjang (skirt cloth)
Central Java
Batik
Cotton
Warp: 226.8 cm.; weft: 103.5 cm.
Costume Council Fund
M.73.73.17

Kain Panjang (skirt cloth)
North coast, Java
Batik
Cotton
Warp: 207.8 cm.; weft: 104.7 cm.
Costume Council Fund
M.73.73.18

Kain Panjang (skirt cloth)
North coast, Java
Batik
Cotton
Warp: 231 cm.; weft: 102.9 cm.
Costume Council Fund
M.73.73.20

Kain Panjang (skirt cloth)
Central Java
Batik
Cotton

Warp: 243 cm.; weft: 102.9 cm.
Costume Council Fund
M.73.73.21

Kain Panjang (skirt cloth)
Central Java
Batik
Cotton
Warp: 246.4 cm.; weft: 104.1 cm.
Costume Council Fund
M.73.73.22

Kain Panjang (skirt cloth)
North coast, Java
Batik
Cotton
Warp: 213.4 cm.; weft: 105.7 cm.
Gift of Mrs. Henry Salvatori
M.73.85.21

Sarong (skirt cloth)
North coast, Java
Batik
Cotton
Warp: 60.9 cm.; weft: 110.5 cm.
Gift of Mrs. Henry Salvatori
M.73.85.22

Kain Panjang (skirt cloth)
Central Java
Batik
Cotton
Warp: 203.2 cm.; weft: 91.4 cm.
Gift of Mrs. A. S. Loebis
CR.74.26.2

Kain Panjang (skirt cloth)
North coast, Java
Batik
Cotton
Warp: 254 cm.; weft: 104.8 cm.
Costume Council Fund
M.77.71.1

Kain Panjang (skirt cloth)
Central Java
Batik
Cotton

Warp: 244.5 cm.; weft: 103.5 cm.
Costume Council Fund
M.77.71.3

Kain Panjang (skirt cloth)
Central Java
Batik
Cotton
Warp: 282.6 cm.; weft: 105.4 cm.
Costume Council Fund
M.77.71.4

Kain Panjang (skirt cloth)
Pekalongan, north coast, Java
Batik
Cotton
Warp: 252.1 cm.; weft: 104.1 cm.
Costume Council Fund
M.77.71.5

Kain Panjang (skirt cloth)
Indramaju, north coast, Java
Batik
Cotton
Warp: 248.3 cm.; weft: 106 cm.
Costume Council Fund
M.77.71.6

Kain Panjang (skirt cloth)
North coast, Java
Batik
Cotton
Warp: 240 cm.; weft: 107.3 cm.
Costume Council Fund
M.77.71.9

Slendang (shoulder cloth)
North coast, Java
Batik
Silk
Warp: 261.3 cm.; weft: 52 cm.
Costume Council Fund
M.77.71.10

Sarong (skirt cloth)
North coast, Java
Batik
Cotton
Warp: 191.8 cm.; weft: 103.5 cm.

Costume Council and Museum
Associates Purchase
M.77.90.2

Sarong (skirt cloth)
North coast, Java
Batik
Cotton
Warp: 203.2 cm.; weft: 105.1 cm.
Costume Council and Museum
Associates Purchase
M.77.90.3

Sarong (skirt cloth)
From the atelier of E. Van Zuylen
Pekalongan, north coast, Java
Batik
Cotton
Warp: 106.4 cm.; weft: 92.1 cm.
Costume Council and Museum
Associates Purchase
M.77.110.1

Kain Panjang (skirt cloth)
Solo, central Java
Batik
Cotton
Warp: 228.6 cm.; weft: 104.8 cm.
Costume Council and Museum
Associates Purchase
M.77.110.2

Kain Panjang (skirt cloth)
North coast, Java
Batik
Cotton
Warp: 228.6 cm.; weft: 104.8 cm.
Costume Council and Museum
Associates Purchase
M.77.110.3

Bali

Slendang (sash)
Bali
Weft ikat
Cotton

Warp: 123.2 cm.; weft: 44.8 cm.
Costume Council Fund
M.73.73.25

Slendang (sash)
Bali
Weft ikat
Silk, metallic threads
Warp: 274.3 cm.; weft: 44.4 cm.
Costume Council Fund
M.74.18.3

Kain Geringsing (sash)
Tenganan, Bali
Double ikat
Cotton
Warp: 191.1 cm.; weft: 59.7 cm.
Costume Council Fund
M.75.73

Kain (skirt cloth)
Bali
Supplementary weft
Silk metallic threads
Warp: 234 cm,.; weft: 74 cm.
Costume Council Fund
M.77.21.1

Kain (skirt cloth)
Bali
Weft ikat
Silk
Warp: 119.3 cm.; weft: 188 cm.
Costume Council Fund
M.77.21.2

Sumba

Slendang (shoulder cloth)
Sumba
Warp ikat
Cotton
Warp: 137.1 cm.; weft: 55.9 cm.
Gift of Mr. Hendrick de Groot
54.25

Hinggi Kombu (man's shawl or waist
cloth)
Melolo-Rende, Sumba

Warp ikat
Cotton
Warp: 248.9 cm.; weft: 120.6 cm.
Costume Council Fund
M.74.19.2

Hinggi Kombu (man's shawl or waist cloth)
Sumba
Warp ikat
Cotton
Warp: 292.1 cm.; weft: 124.4 cm.
Gift of Steven G. Alpert
M.77.104

Woman's Funeral Costume
Rende, Sumba
Tortoiseshell Comb
Height: 15.2 cm.; width: 17.4 cm.
Breast Ornament
Height: 40.7 cm.; width: 22.2 cm.
Lau (woman's skirt cloth)
Height: 97.8 cm.; width: 32.3 cm.
Carrying Bag
Height: 24.1 cm.; width: 19.7 cm.
Knee Ornaments
Length: 29.9 cm.; width: .63 cm.
Costume Council Fund
M.77.91a-g

Lau (woman's skirt cloth)
Melolo, Sumba
Warp ikat, supplementary warp
Cotton
Warp: 167.7 cm.; weft: 124.4 cm.
Costume Council and Museum Associates Purchase
TR.2188.1

Flores

Sarong (skirt cloth)
Lio, Flores
Warp ikat
Cotton
Warp: 136 cm.; weft: 171.4 cm.
Costume Council Fund
M.73.73.11

Sarong (skirt cloth)
Lio area, Flores
Warp ikat
Cotton
Warp: 141 cm.; weft: 190.5 cm.
Costume Council and Museum Associates Purchase
M.77.93.1

Slendang (shoulder cloth)
Lio, Flores
Warp ikat
Cotton
Warp: 163.8 cm.; weft: 62.2 cm.
Costume Council Fund
M.77.93.3

Roti

Slendang (shoulder cloth)
Roti
Warp ikat
Cotton
Warp: 99 cm.; weft: 43.1 cm.
Gift of Verra Darwiko
M.77.84

Sarong (skirt cloth)
Roti
Warp ikat
Cotton
Warp: 114.3 cm.; weft: 141 cm.
Costume Council Fund
M.77.81.28

Timor

Man's Sash
Niki, Timor
Weft twining, tapestry weave
Cotton, beads, metallic ornaments
Warp: 193 cm.; weft: 20.3 cm.
Costume Council Fund
M.77.81.29

General

Alkema, B., and Bezemer, T. J., *Beknopt Handboek der Bolkenkunde van Nederlandsch-Indië,* 1927.

Bühler, Alfred, "The Essentials of Handicrafts and the Craft of Weaving among Primitive People," *Ciba Review,* no. 30, 1941.

Bühler, Alfred, "The Ikat Technique," *Ciba Review,* no. 44, 1942.

"Dyeing among Primitive Peoples," *Ciba Review,* no. 68, 1948.

Haar, B. te , *Adat Law in Indonesia,* New York: Institute of Pacific Relations, 1948

Indonesian Ornamental Design, Bandung, 1949.

Indonesische Gewebe, exhibition catalog, Basel: Gewerbemuseum, 1947.

Indonesische Textilkunst, Vienna: Museum für Völkerkunde, 1964.

Jasper, J. E., and Pirngadie, Mas, *De Weefkunst,* vol. 2 of *De Inlandsche kunstnijverheid in Nederlandsche-Indië,* The Hague: Mouton and Co., 1912.

Kennedy, R., *Bibliography of Indonesian Peoples and Cultures,* revised and edited by T. W. Maretzki and H. T. Fischer, New Haven, 1962.

Langewis, Laurens, and Wagner, Frits A., *Decorative Art in Indonesian Textiles,* Amsterdam: C.P. J. van der Peet, 1964.

Larsen, Jack Lenor, with Bühler, Alfred; Solyom, Bronwen; and Solyom, Garrett, *The Dyer's Art: Ikat, Batik, Plangi,* New York: Van Nostrand Reinhold, 1976.

Maxwell, John R., and Maxwell, Robyn J., *Textiles of Indonesia: An Introductory Handbook,* Indonesian Arts Society in association with the National Gallery of Victoria, 1976.

Murdock, G., *Social Structure in Southeast Asia,* New York, 1960.

Nieuwenhuis, A. W., *Die Veranlagung der Malaiischen Völker des Ost-Indischen Archipels: Erläutert an ihren Industriellen Erzeugnissen,* Internationales Archiv für Ethnographie, supplement to vol. 21, Leiden: E. J. Brill, 1913.

Paravicini, E., *Batik und Ikat,* exhibition catalog, Basel: Gewerbemuseum, 1924.

Solyom, Garrett, and Solyom, Bronwen, *Textiles of the Indonesian Archipelago,* Asian Studies at Hawaii, no. 10, Honolulu: University Press of Hawaii, 1973.

Spegel, H., "Soul-Boats in Melanesia: A Study in Diffusion," *Archaeology and Physical Anthropology of Oceania,* vol. 6, no. 1, 1971, pp. 34-43.

Thomassen à Thuessink van der Hoop, A.N.J., *Indonesische siermotieven,* Jakarta: Koninklijk Bataviaasch genootschap van kunsten en wetenschappen, 1949.

Turner, Victor, *The Forest of Symbols,* Ithaca: Cornell University Press, 1967.

Wagner, Frits A., *Indonesia, the Art of an Island Group,* New York: McGraw-Hill, 1959.

Sumatra

Bühler, Alfred, "Turkey Red Dyeing in South and South East Asia," *Ciba Review,* no. 39, 1941, pp. 1423-26.

Bühler, Alfred, "Plangi—The Tie and Dye Work," *Ciba Review,* no. 104, 1954.

Bühler, Alfred, "Patola Influences in Southeast Asia," *Journal of Indian Textile History,* vol. 4, 1959, pp. 4-46.

Gittinger, Mattiebelle, unpublished field notes, 1970.

Gittinger, Mattiebelle, "A Study of the Ship Cloths of South Sumatra: Their Design and Usage," doctoral dissertation (unpublished), Columbia University, New York, 1972.

Gittinger, Mattiebelle, "Selected Batak Textiles: Technique and Function," *Textile Museum Journal,* vol. 4, no. 2, 1975, pp. 13-29.

Gittinger, Mattiebelle, "The Ship Textiles of South Sumatra: Functions and Design System," *Bijdragen tot de Taal-, Land- en Volkenkunde,* vol. 132, nos. 2 and 3, 1976, pp. 207-27.

Hille, J. W. van, "Het vervaardiging der kain tjermoek in de afdeeling Kauer (residentie Benkoelen)," *Tijdschrift voor Nijverheid en Landbouw,* vol. 48, 1894, pp. 178-80.

Nabholz-Kartaschoff, Marie-Louise, *Plangi,* Basel: Museum für Völkerkunde, 1969.

Obdeyn, V., "Indragirische weefkunst," *Tijdschrift van het Koninklijk Bataviaasch genootschap van kunsten en wetenschappen,* vol. 48, nos. 1 and 2, 1929, pp. 92-124.

op't Land, C., "Een merkwaardige 'Tampan pengantar' van Zuid-Sumatra," *Kultuurpatronen,* vol. 10, 1968-69, pp. 100-117.

Palm, C.H.M., "De cultuur en kunst van de Lampung, Sumatra," *Kultuurpatronen,* vol. 7, 1965, pp. 40-79.

Steinmann, Alfred, "Les 'tissus à jonques' de sud de Sumatra," *Revue des arts asiatiques,* vol. 11, 1937, pp. 131-43.

Toorn, J. L. van der, "Aanteekeningen uit het familieleven bij den Maleiers in de Padangsche bovenlanden," *Tijdschrift van Indische Taal-, Land- en Volkenkunde,* vol. 26, 1881, pp. 205-28 and 514-28.

Veltman, Th. J., "De Atjehsche zijdeindustrie," *Internationales Archiv für Ethnographie,* vol. 20, 1912, pp. 16-58.

Vergouwen, J. C., *The Social Organization and Customary Law of the Toba-Batak of Northern Sumatra,* The Hague: Martinus Nijhoff, 1964, originally published in 1933.

Borneo

Haddon, Alfred C., and Start, Laura E., *Iban or Sea Dayak Fabrics and Their Patterns,* Cambridge: The University Press, 1936.

Heine-Geldern, Robert von, introduction to *Indonesian Art,* exhibition catalog, Royal Indies Institute, Amsterdam, New York: The Asia Institute, 1948.

Hose, Charles, and McDougall, William, *The Pagan Tribes of Borneo,* 2 vols., London, 1912.

Jensen, Erik, *The Iban and Their Religion,* Oxford: Clarendon Press, 1974.

Loeber, J.A., Jr., *Het Weven in Nederlandsch-Indië,* Amsterdam, 1903.

Roth, Henry Ling, *The Natives of Sarawak and British North Borneo,* 2 vols., London, 1896, reprinted, Kuala Lumpur: University of Malaya Press, 1968.

Schuster, Carl, "Remarks on the Design of an Early *Ikat* Textile in Japan," *Festschrift Alfred Bühler,* Basler Beiträge zur Geographie und Ethnologie, Ethnologische Reihe, vol. 2, 1965.

Celebes

Downs, Richard Erskine, *The Religion of the Bare'e-Speaking Toradja of Central Celebes,* The Hague, 1956.

Jager Gerlings, J. H., *Sprekende Weefsels,* Amsterdam: Scheltens and Giltay, 1952.

Kooijman, S., *Ornamented Bark-Cloth in Indonesia,* Leiden: E. J. Brill, 1963.

Kruyt, Alb. C., *De West-Toradjas op Midden-Celebes,* Platen Atlas, Amsterdam, 1938.

Nooy-Palm, C.H.M., *De karbouw en de kandaure,* Delft: Indonesisch Ethnografisch Museum, 1975.

Nooy-Palm, C.H.M., "Dress and Adornment of the Sa'dan-Toradja (Celebes, Indonesia)," *Tropical Man,* vol. 2, Leiden: E.J. Brill, 1969.

Nouhuys, J. W. van, "Een autochthoon weefgebied in Midden-Celebes," *Nederlandsch-Indië Oud en Nieuw,* 6th year, no. 8, December 1921.

Nouhuys, J. W. van, "Was-Batik in Midden-Celebes," *Nederlandsch-Indië Oud en Nieuw,* 10th year, no. 4, August 1925.

Schuster, Carl, "Remarks on the Design of an Early *Ikat* Textile in Japan," *Festschrift Alfred Bühler,* Basler Beit-

räge zur Geographie und Ethnologie, Ethnologische Reihe, vol. 2, 1965.

Java

Adam, Tassilo, "The Art of Batik in Java," *Bulletin of the Needle and Bobbin Club,* vol. 18, nos. 1-2, 1934, pp. 2-79.

Adams, Marie Jeanne, "Symbolic Scenes in Javanese Batik," *Textile Museum Journal,* vol. 3, no. 1, 1970, pp. 25-40.

Batiks, Victoria and Albert Museum, London: H.M.S.O., 1969.

Bolland, Rita; Jager Gerlings, J.H.; and Langewis, Laurens, *Batiks from Java: The Refined Beauty of an Ancient Craft,* 3 vols., Amsterdam: Koninklijk Instituut voor de Tropen, Department of Cultural and Physical Anthropology, 1960.

Damais, S.J.H., *Batik,* Jakarta: Municipal Committee of PATA 74, 1974.

Hurwitz, J., *Batikkunst van Java,* Rotterdam: Museum voor Land- en Volkenkunde, 1962.

Jasper, J.E., and Pirngadie, Mas, *De batikkunst,* vol. 3 of *De inlandsche kunstnijverheid in Nederlandsche-Indië,* The Hague: Mouton and Co., 1916.

Marzuki, Jazir; Tirtaamidjaja, N.; and Anderson, Benedict R. O'G., *Batik: pola dan tjorak—Pattern and Motif,* Jakarta: Jambatan, 1966.

Nabholz-Kartaschoff, Marie-Louise, *Batik: Formen und Verbreitung eines Reserveverfahrens zur Musterung von Textilien,* Basel: Museum für Völkerkunde und Schweizerisches Museum für Volkskunde, 1970.

Rouffaer, G.P., and Juynboll, H. H., *De batik-kunst in Nederlandsch-Indië en haar geschiedenis*, 2 vols., Publicaties van 's Rijks Ethnographisch Museum, series 2, no. 1, Haarlem: H. Kleinmann, 1900.

Steinmann, Alfred, "Batiks," *Ciba Review*, no. 58, 1947, 2090-2125.

Steinmann, Alfred, *Batik: A Survey of Batik Design*, Leigh-on-Sea: F. Lewis, 1958.

Tirta, Iwan, and Lau, Raymond, *Batik, the Magic Cloth*, n.p., 1974.

Veldhuisen-Djajasoebrata, Alit, *Batik op Java*, Rotterdam: Museum voor Land- en Volkenkunde, 1972.

Wagner, Frits A., *Batikkunst in Indonesie*, typescript, Haarlem, October 1949.

Bali

Aussereuropäische Textilien, Sammlungs-katalog 2, Zurich: Kunstgewerbe-museum, n.d.

Bolland, Rita, "A Comparison between the Looms Used in Bali and Lombok for Weaving Sacred Cloths," *Tropical Man*, 1971, vol. 4, pp. 171-82.

Bühler, Alfred, "The Ikat Technique," *Ciba Review*, no. 44, 1942, 1586-96.

Bühler, Alfred, *Materialien zur Kenntnis der Ikattechnik: Definition und Bezeich-nungen, Geschichtliches, mechanische Verarbeitung des Garnes*, Internationales Archiv für Ethnographie, supplement to vol. 43, Leiden: E. J. Brill, 1943.

Bühler, Alfred, "Patola Influences in Southeast Asia," *Journal of Indian Textile History*, no. 4, 1959, pp. 4-46.

Bühler, Alfred; Ramseyer, Urs; and Ramseyer-Gygi, Nicole, *Patola und Geringsing: Zeremonialtucher aus Indien und Indonesien*, Basel: Museum für Völkerkunde und Schweizerisches Museum für Volkskunde/Soncherausstellung, 1975-76.

Covarrubias, Miguel, *The Island of Bali*, New York: Knopf, 1965.

Goris, R., *Bali: Atlas Kebudayaan*, n.p., Pemerintah Republic Indonesia, n.d.

Korn, Victor Emanuel, "The Village Republic of Tenganan Pegeringsingan," in *Bali: Studies in Life, Thought and Ritual*, pp. 301-68, The Hague: W. van Hoeve, 1960.

Langewis, Laurens, "A Woven Balinese Lamak," in *Lamak and Malat in Bali and a Sumba Loom* (no. CXIX, Department of Cultural and Physical Anthropology, no. 53), Amsterdam: Royal Tropical Institute, 1956, pp. 31-47.

Mershon, Katharane Edson, *Seven plus Seven: Mysterious Life-Rituals in Bali*, New York: Vantage, 1971.

Pelras, Christian, "Tissage balinais," *Objets et mondes*, vol. 2, no. 4, 1962, pp. 215-40.

Pelras, Christian, "Lamak et tissus sacrés de Bali," *Objets et mondes*, vol. 7, no. 4, 1967, pp. 255-78.

Wirz, Paul, "Die Magischen Gewebe von Bali und Lombok," *Jahrbuch des Bernischen Historischen Museums*, no. 11, 1931, pp. 129-39.

de Zoete, Beryl, and Spies, Walter, *Dance and Drama in Bali*, Kuala Lumpur: Oxford University Press, 1973.

Sumba

Adams, Marie Jeanne, *Leven en dood op Sumba, Life and Death on Sumba*, exhibi-tion catalog, Rotterdam: Museum voor Land- en Volkenkunde, 1965-66.

Adams, Marie Jeanne, "Tissus décorés de l'île de Sumba," *Objets et mondes*, vol. 6, 1966, pp. 3-18.

Adams, Marie Jeanne, *System and Meaning in East Sumba Textile Design: A Study in Traditional Indonesian Art*, Southeast Asia Studies Cultural Report Series, no. 16, New Haven: Yale University, 1969.

Adams, Marie Jeanne, "Indonesian Textiles at the Textile Museum," *Textile Museum Journal*, vol. 3, no. 1, 1970, pp. 41-44.

Adams, Marie Jeanne, "Designs in Sumba Textiles, Local Meanings and Foreign Influences," *Textile Museum Journal*, vol. 3, no. 2, 1971, pp. 28-37.

Adams, Marie Jeanne, "Tiedying, an Art on the Island of Sumba," *Handweaver and Craftsman*, vol. 22, 1971, pp. 9-11 and 37.

Adams, Marie Jeanne, "Classic and Eccentric Elements in East Sumba Textiles," *Needle and Bobbin Club Bulletin*, vol. 55, 1972, pp. 3-40.

Alphen, H. J., "Soemba en de Soem-baneezen," *Tijdschrift voor Nederlandsch-Indië*, vol. 1, 1884, pp. 205-8.

Nieuwenkamp, W., "Soemba-Weefsels," *Tijdschrift van het Koninklijk Neder-landsche aardrijkskundig genootschap*, vol. 37, 1920, pp. 374-89 and 503-13.

Nieuwenkamp, W., "Iets over Soemba en de Soemba weefsels," *Nederlandsch-Indië, Oud en Nieuw*, vol. 7, 1922-23, pp. 295-313.

Nieuwenkamp, W., "Eenige voorbeelden van het ornament op de weefsels van Soemba" (catalog of part of the Nieuwenkamp collection), *Nederlandsch-Indië, Oud en Nieuw*, vol. 11, 1926-27, pp. 259-88.

Nooteboom, C., *Oost-Soemba: een volkenkundige studie*, The Hague, 1940.

Ouwehand, C., "Adatrecht en Daerah-wetgeving met betrekking tot de bos-bescherming op Soemba," *Indonesie*, vol. 4, 1951, pp. 536-49.

Real, Daniel, "Tissus des Indes Néerlan-daises," 49 plates of textiles from the Nieuwenkamp collection shown at the *Exposition de l'art décoratif aux Indes Néerlandaises*, Musée des Arts Décoratifs, Paris, 1927.

Von Koenigswald, G., "Sumba and Ordos," *Kultuurpatronen*, vols. 3-4, 1961, pp. 120-23.

Roti, Ndao, and Savu

Bühler, Alfred, "Die Herstellung von Ikattüchern auf der Insel Rote," *Verhandlungen der Naturforschenden Gesellschaft von Basel*, vol. 50, 1939, pp. 32-97.

Fox, James J., *Harvest of the Palm*, Cambridge: Harvard University Press, 1977.